THE PHILIP MORRIS COLLECTION

established by the
Virginia Foundation for Independent Colleges

IN DEEP APPRECIATION
FOR THE GENEROUS SUPPORT
OF ITS MEMBER INSTITUTIONS

by

Philip Morris Companies Inc.

RICHARD M. NIXON

GARLAND REFERENCE LIBRARY
OF SOCIAL SCIENCE
(Vol. 415)

RICHARD M. NIXON
A Bibliographic Exploration

Dale E. Casper

GARLAND PUBLISHING, INC. • NEW YORK & LONDON
1988

Library of Congress Cataloging-in-Publication Data

Casper, Dale E.
Richard M. Nixon: A Bibliographic Exploration / by Dale E.
Casper.
p. cm.—(Garland Reference Library of Social Science; v.
415)
Includes index.
ISBN 0–8240–8478–0
1. Nixon, Richard M. (Richard Milhous), 1913– —Bibliography.
2. United States—Politics and government—1969–1974—Bibliography.
I. Title. II. Series.

Z8629.4.C37 1988 [E856] 973.924′092′4—dc19 87–28064 CIP

Printed on acid-free, 250-year-life paper
Manufactured in the United States of America

TO JARED, MY SON

CONTENTS

PREFACE

Many valuable past works have assisted in the tracing
of citations used in this bibliography. I would like to
acknowledge my indebtedness to all those authors who have
written about Richard Nixon and then took the time to list
their sources of information. A special thanks to Richard
Chapin, director of libraries at Michigan State University,
who allowed me the needed flexibility in work time in order
that the gathering of citations included in this book could
occur. Also, sincere good wishes to John Hazard, Assistant
Secretary of Transportation in the Nixon Administration, who
provided several personal reflections on Richard Nixon and
his presidential administration which added to my own
understanding of the man and the time period.

Richard M. Nixon

A Place in History: An Assessment of the Nixon Literature

In 1968, Richard Nixon became the first vice-president
to be elected president without succeeding the president he
had served.   In 1972, Richard Nixon became the first
presidential candidate to carry forty-nine of the fifty
states in a successful election to the presidency.   In 1974,
Richard Nixon became the first president to resign his
office.   Victory can be but momentary in the expanse of time
which forms the record of human history.   Richard Nixon's
political career is a contrast of victory and defeat.   he
lost the 1960 presidential election although he gained the
highest popular vote total ever won by a losing candidate.[1]
In 1968, Nixon reversed the 1960 election result by
defeating Hubert Humphrey by the smallest margin since his
own loss in 1960.[2]   The Nixon slush fund scandal revealed
during the 1952 presidential election campaign would have
caused Nixon to be dumped from the Republican Party ticket
as vice-president except for his brilliant televised
"Checkers speech."[3]   Twenty-two years later, the Watergate
scandal revealed shortly after the 1972 presidential
election campaign did cause Nixon to be dumped from the
presidency after the televised hearings of the Senate Select

1

Committee investigating the scandal had added greatly to the impeachment atmosphere that forced Nixon to resign.

For over twenty-five years, Richard Nixon was visible on the American political scene. Nixon's rise from the Red scare of the late 1940s[4] to be the most obvious candidate to succeed Dwight D. Eisenhower in the presidency is unique. A relatively unknown California politician from an impoverished family background became vice-president of the United States within six years of his first campaigning for political office. Eight years after his election as vice-president, Nixon was so entrenched in the Republican Party that there was no other candidate strong enough to oppose his nomination as the presidential candidate.[5] The record of Nixon's early political career is just as spotted with glorious achievement and dismal defeat as his later years as president. Victory at the polls in congressional races over strong liberal Democratic candidates with national followings helped Nixon to become the Republican vice-presidential candidate. But, the Nixon slush fund scandal revealed early in the fall of 1952 embarrassed Dwight Eisenhower sufficiently for the general to suggest that Nixon withdraw as his vice-presidential running mate. Successfully managing the U.S. executive branch during Eisenhouwer's first heart attack earned Nixon praise from the press but also brought questions about Eisenhower's support for Nixon to again be his vice-presidential

candidate in the 1956 election.[6] Campaigning hard for the
Republican Party in the 1950s earned Nixon the lead place on
the 1960 presidential ticket but raised doubts and
reservations about his fitness for the presidency among the
media. Nixon, indeed, was condemned for what he did and
what he did not do in the early part of his political
career.

Controversy, which seemed to find Nixon throughout his
life in American politics, also contributed greatly to the
record of literature about Richard Nixon. Twenty-five years
of political events that often involved conflict and debate
among political analysts guaranteed frequent political
commentary, analysis, and critical review that many
publications regard as the core of their intellectual
content. Added to this body of political analysis is the
voluminous reporting of the events in which Nixon was
directly or indirectly involved. Presidents, vice-
presidents, and presidential candidates are news producers.
Coverage of such figures is frequent even if disportionate
to the importance of the event. The Nixon literature is
enormous in quantity, critical to an understanding of many
significant American and international developments, and
interwoven with the social and psychological themes of the
American people during the Cold War period.

The events, the politically important offices involved,

and the volume of the literature available suggest that
Richard Nixon has a continuing role in the interpretation
and analysis of American twentieth century history. Former
presidents are usually concerned that their administrations
are remembered for great deeds accomplished and good
leadership provided. But, history continues beyond any
presidential tenure, and historians are often unkind in
their appraisals of presidential performance. That Richard
Nixon has earned a place in the historical memory of the
American nation is a certainty. For generations, students
of American history will learn the appropriate response to
the question of interpretation of Nixon's influence on the
course of American history during the later part of the
twentieth century. Will Nixon be remembered for political
scandal and defeat of such magnitude that American politics
changed?[7] Will Nixon be remembered for understanding
America's limitations in the world and thus the last
president to provide a coherent approach to the conduct of
world affairs?[8] Will Nixon be remembered as the last
effective liberal president who was succeeded by a number of
conservative ideologues who changed the American consensus
on social and foreign policy created during the New Deal
era?[9] Will Nixon be remembered for his influence on
subsequent historical events or only as a good trivia
question item?

Richard Nixon's continuing influence can be recorded

through a perusal of leading popular and scholarly
periodicals. Since 1974 Nixon has been the subject of 396
articles listed in the Readers Guide to Periodical
Literature, which indexes the 200 most popularly read
magazines published. It is interesting to note that over
one-third of those articles were written after 1980.
More scholarly articles about Richard Nixon have been just
as abundant. Since 1980, by the record maintained in the
Social Sciences Citation Index, 246 articles have been
published with reference to Richard Nixon. The average
number of popular and scholarly articles written about Nixon
since 1980 is, thus, over 40 per year. The content of
these periodical articles is revealing with regard to the
historical memory of Nixon's presidency. A review of the
scholarly articles written about Richard Nixon since 1975 in
Presidential Studies Quarterly, American Political Science
Review, Political Science Quarterly, and the Journal of
Politics indicate that less than 50 percent of these relate
to the Watergate scandal and Nixon's resignation of the
presidency. The other articles focus upon policies and
actions taken by the Nixon administration in the area of
domestic or foreign affairs.[10] Watergate is significant but
so are other aspects of the Nixon presidency if an
assessment is to be made based upon content of scholarly
research.

A nation's culture and history are passed from one
generation to another through educational institutions. In
the early 1980s, Richard Nixon achieved themes of American
history. Comparison with succeeding presidents has allowed
the Nixon administration to emerge from the weight of the
Watergate scandal and be judged on the merit of its domestic
and foreign policies. Though Nixon was labelled a
conservative by his political opponents, many domestic and
foreign initiatives undertaken by his presidency were
considered liberal actions even at the time that they
occurred. Nixon's proposal to provide a minimum guaranteed
income to welfare familes,[11] his use of wage and price
controls,[12] and his opening of China to U.S. businessmen and
visitors[13] were all considered as liberal political actions.
With academia some maintained in the early 1980s that
Richard Nixon as president personally accepted the social
legislation enacted by liberal presidents since the New Deal
era and that he acted only to curb the excesses of Johnson's
Great Society, which was based upon the premise that social,
political, and economic problems could be overcome through
federal expenditures. A review of the textbooks used in
college-level American history courses confirms this
reappraisal of the Nixon administration within the nation's
professoriat.[14]

In 1976, James Patterson's America in the Twentieth
Century was available for use in college-level American

history courses as a core textbook for teaching American history. In fact, Princeton University was using this work to teach American history in 1982.[15] Patterson's narrative of the events surrounding the Nixon presidency is unsympathetic. He lists Nixon's style, domestic policies, so-called southern strategy for maintaining political support, and the U.S. involvement in Vietnam as reasons for judging the Nixon presidency as a failure. Richard Nixon remains, in Patterson's book, the villain whom the Watergate scandal hysteria had created in 1974. Even the area most viewed by objective critics as a success for the Nixon presidency, foreign affairs, is labelled as a failure by James Patterson. By 1981 an alternative viewpoint to Patterson's was available for use in college-level American history courses when The Great Republic: A History of the American People by Bernard Bailyn was published in a revised edition. The image of the Nixon presidency contained within The Great Republic is well revealed in this quote "There was little warmth in his political style, but Nixon proved to be an extraordinarily successful president during this first term." Many of Nixon's policies as president are praised. Nixon's foreign policy is labelled "exceptional." His economic actions are labelled as "dramatic moves" to counter inflation and recession. The Great Republic interprets the Watergate scandal as a personal problem for Richard Nixon

that ended his presidency prematurely. Richard Nixon in the
Great Republic suffered punishment for his personal sin of
pride. Numerous college-level American history courses have
adopted the Great Republic. In 1982, the University of
North Carolina at Chapel Hill was one such educational
institution.[16]

It is remarkable that in the annals of American history
a discredited politician has been allowed to regain
respectability within his lifetime. Many U.S. political
figures have endured public humiliation and vilification
while in political office and then have been granted
respectability as a political sage by a future generation of
scholars. Harry Truman serves as a recent example of this
fact. But Richard Nixon, who was accused of numerous
political crimes leading to impeachment proceedings in the
House of Representatives, who was hated and detested by a
generation of young Americans for his support of the U.S.
involvement in Vietnam, and who was viewed by many as a
monarch trampling on every cherished tenet of the American
political process has seen his administration as president
of the United States reappraised and given significant
praise even while he still lives in retirement. This factor
is key to a continuing influence for Richard Nixon in the
debates about American domestic and foreign policies.
Richard Nixon still captures the imagination of the American
people.[17] His skills at diplomacy and the manipulation of

political events[18] have earned him a lasting place in the
common memory of the American nation and guarantee him an
objective hearing before each generation of historians and
political analysts who conduct research into the momentous
events associated with his political career.[19]

Notes

1. The popular vote totals were Kennedy 34,221,349 and
Nixon 34,108,647.

2. The popular vote totals were Nixon 313,770,237 and
Humphrey 31,270,533.

3. See Henry F. McGuckin, "A Value Analysis of Richard
Nixon's 1952 Campaign Fund Speech." Southern Speech Journal
33 (Summer 1968): 259-269; Arthur E. Rowse, Slanted News: A
Case Study of the Nixon and Stevenson Fund Stories. Boston,
MA: Beacon Press, 1957; "Defense of Checkers." Commweal 57
(October 10, 1952): 3; and Garry Wills "The Checkers
Speech." Esquire 99 (June 1983): 122-124+.

4. See Paul Bullock, "Rabbits and Radicals: Richard
Nixon's 1946 Campaign Against Jerry Voorhis." Southern
California Quarterly 55 (Fall 1973): 319-359; Ingrid W.
Scobie, "Helen Gahagen Douglas and Her 1950 Senate Race with
Richard M. Nixon." Southern California Quarterly 58 (Spring
1976): 113-126; and Harry W. Flannery, "Red Smear in
California." Commonweal 53 (December 8, 1950): 225.

5. See Theodore White, The Making of the President,
1960. New York, NY: Atheneum, 1961.

6. See "Will Nixon Be on the Ticket Again?" U.S.
News and World Report 41 (August 10, 1956): 25-28.

7. See Theodore L. Becker "Watergate: On Campaigns and
Government Anarchy." Society 10 (July 1973): 12-13; David
Adamany and George Agree "Election Campaign Financing: The
1974 Reforms." Political Science Quarterly 90 (Summer 1975:
201-220; Jack M. McLeod "Watergate and the 1974
Congressional Election." Public Opinion Quarterly 41
(Summer 1977): 181-195.

8. Cyrus L. Sulzberger (The World and Richard Nixon.
Englewood Cliffs, NJ: Prentice-Hall, 1987) makes this point
quite well.

9. A. James Reichley's Conservatives in an Age of Change:
The Nixon and Ford Administration (Washington, DC:
Brookings Institution, 1981) makes a good case for this
point.

10. Significant non-Watergate-related articles are: Joel
D. Aberbach and Bert A. Rochman, "Clashing Beliefs Within
the Executive Branch: The Nixon Administration
Bureaucracy." American Political Science Review 70 (June
1976): 452-468; Richard L. Cole and David A. Caputo,
"Presidential Control of the Senior Civil Service: Assessing
the Strategies of the Nixon Years." American Political
Science Review 73 (June 1979): 399-413; and James D.
Calder, "Presidents and Crime Control: Kennedy, Johnson,
and Nixon and the Influences of Ideology." Presidential
Studies Quarterly 12 (Fall 1982): 574-589.

11. See Vincent Burke, Nixon's Good Deed: Welfare Reform.
New York, NY: Columbia University Press, 1974.

12. See Roger L. Miller and Raburn M. Williams, The New
Economics of Richard Nixon: Freezes, Floats, and Fiscal
Policy. New York, NY: Harper and Row, 1972.

13. See Gargi Dutti, "China and the Shift in Superpower
Relations." International Studies 13 (October 1974): 635-
622 and Morton A. Kaplan, The Nixon Initiative and Chinese
American Relations. Edwardsville, IL: Southern Illinois
University Press, 1972.

14. A review of the content of college-level American
history courses is presented in Warren Susman and John
Chambers, American History: Selected Reading Lists and
Course Outlines from American Colleges and Universities.
New York, NY: Markus Publishing Inc., 1983.

15. Ibid., vol. III, p. 41.

16. Ibid., Vol. I, p. 20.

17. An examination of this is presented in Steven R.
Brown, "Richard Nixon and the Public Conscience: The
Struggle for Authenticity." Journal of Psychohistory 6
(Summer 1976): 93-111.

18. An example of this is seen in the suggestion made in early 1987 by the governor of New York, Mario Cuomo, that Richard Nixon be sent to negotiate a new arms limitation treaty with the Soviet Union based upon his past experience at negotiations with the Soviets.

19. Stephen E. Ambrose, <u>Nixon: The Education of a President, 1913-1962</u> (New York, NY: Simon and Schuster, 1987) is a recent example of an objective assessment of Nixon's early political career.

A Guide to the Use of the Bibliography

This bibliography is not all inclusive. Richard
Nixon's career in American politics spans a twenty-five year
period. In addition to the books and journal articles
written about Nixon, there are countless government
documents encompassing Nixon's activities as vice-president
and president. These documents alone would constitute a
significant bibliography. A selective compilation of books
and journal articles that examine the events relevant to
Richard Nixon's career in politics and presidential
administration constitute the body of this bibliography.
There are over 1700 citations provided; these will serve as
a beginning guide for research into the relevant topics
associated with Richard Nixon.

Recent research was an important guideline for gathering
the citations listed. However, the usefulness of this
bibliography is affected by other publications that have
appeared even before the bibliography is printed and
available for consultation. For all bibliographic chapters
the years covered include that of the event/topic presented
until 1986. The chapters concerned with works relating to
the biography and campaigns of Richard Nixon date from the
late 1940s to 1986. The only time limitation used in the
gathering of citations for the bibliography was that imposed

by the chronological dates of Nixon's life.

The citations listed in the bibliography are limited to the works in the English language. There are, however, a number of relevant studies relating to Richard Nixon published in foreign languages. These studies can be located by various abstracts and indexes concerned with American history, politics, and the social sciences in general. The process of gathering citations for the bibliography revealed several important foreign language publications relating to Richard Nixon. These works should be reviewed by the serious researcher of Nixon materials in order to gain a comparative analysis of important events in Nixon's political career.

Topical divisions of the Nixon literature can be accomplished in several different ways depending upon the view of Nixon's life and/or political career presented. The arrangement of this bibliography is based upon a decision to highlight the major achievements of Nixon's career in American politics and provide a focal point for a significant narrative and analytical works that are representative of those written on the topic presented.

Structure of this Bibliography

The bibliography has five parts. The general introduction to the Nixon literature is followed by a review of the abstracts, indexes, and periodicals used in compiling this bibliography. Next comes the body of citations relating to the political career of Richard Nixon. Finally, a name and subject index provides additional access to the items listed in the bibliographic section of the work.

All citations have been assigned a number. These numbers begin with the biography chapter and continue to the end of the bibliography. Each citation follows standard form. Books are cited with author's name, title, place of publication, and date of publication or copyright. Periodical citations include author's name, title of article, title of periodical, volume number, the date of issue, and pagination.

Abstracts and Indexes

Several services provide indexing and abstracts for literature relating to Richard Nixon and the American presidency in general. In addition, subject headings such as U.S.--History, U.S.--Politics and Government, and U.S.--Presidents, will locate relevant information in indexes and abstracts that cover broad subject fields in the social and behavioral sciences as well as history. The following

titles in indexes and abstracts are representative of those
providing the most useful assess to recent research on the
political career and presidency of Richard M. Nixon that has
been published in books, journals, and conference
proceedings.

American History and Life: A Guide to Periodical
    Literature. Santa Barbara, CA: ABC-CLIO Press,
    1964-   ; quarterly.

U.S. and Canadian history are the focus of this guide
to recent literature. There are four major sections to this
publication. The most useful for locating information about
Richard Nixon are parts A and B. Part A is a listing of
abstracts and bibliographic citations from over 1500 U.S.,
Canadian, and European periodicals. It also contains
abstracts and citations organized into geographic categories
that are further subdivided chronologically. A subject
index is provided for Part A. Useful subject headings are
Richard M. Nixon, Presidency, and Presidents. Part B is a
listing of book reviews accessed through either an author or
subject index provided.

Biography Index. New York, NY: H.W. Wilson Company,
    1946- ; quarterly.

A comprehensive index to biographical materials
published in periodicals, books, collective works, and
incidental biographical material in non-biographical works,

Biography Index includes obituaries, collections of letters, diaries, memoirs, and bibliographies. The index is arranged alphabetically by the name of the biographees. Richard M. Nixon is the appropriate subject heading.

Humanities Index. New York, NY: H.W. Wilson Company,
    1974- ; quarterly.

Humanities Index is a cumulative index to the subjects of archaeology, classical studies, area studies, folklore, history, language and literature, the performing arts, philosophy, religion and theology, and other related subjects appearing in English-language periodicals. The index consists of author and subject entries arranged alphabetically. The most useful subject headings are Richard M. Nixon, United States--History, United States-- Politics and Government, and Presidents--United States.

International Political Science Abstracts. Paris, France:
    International Political Science Association,
    1951- ; bimonthly.

International Political Science Abstracts is a listing of non-evaluative abstracts of journal articles published in the field of political science throughout the world. Abstracts are in English and French. Useful subject headings are Richard M. Nixon and United States--Presidents.

<u>Political Science Abstracts Annual Supplement</u>. New York,
    NY: Plenum Publishing Corporation, 1967-; annual.

The annual supplement to <u>Political Science Abstracts</u>
contains abstracts of materials relating to politics and
political analysis from public affairs magazines, major
newspapers, professional journals, and books. The index to
the <u>Annual Supplement</u> contains numerous subject headings
arranged alphabetically. After each subject heading is a
reference to page and entry number for the listing of the
abstracts which are arranged numerically. Nixon/R is the
appropriate subject heading for this index.

<u>Public Affairs Information Service Bulletin</u> (PAIS). New
    York, NY: Public Information Service, Inc., 1913- ;
    semi-monthly.

A classified index to books, journal articles,
pamphlets, reports, government publications, publications of
significant societies and associations, and government
legislation, <u>Public Affairs Information Service Bulletin</u>
provides access to information on economics, social
conditions, and public affairs in general. Useful subject
headings relating to materials on Richard Nixon are Richard
Milhous Nixon and United States--President.

Readers Guide to Periodical Literature. New York, NY: H.W.
     Wilson Company, 1900-   ; quarterly.

A cumulative index to periodicals of general interest
in the United States, Readers Guide consists of subject and
author entries arranged in one alphabet. Among the useful
subject headings are Richard M. Nixon, United States--
History, United States--Politics and Government, and
Presidents.

Social Sciences and Humanities Index. New York, NY: H.W.
     Wilson Company, 1907-1974; quarterly.

Social Sciences and Humanities Index is an author and
subject index to English-language periodicals covering the
subjects of anthropology, archaeology, area studies,
classical studies, economics, geography, history, language
and literature, philosophy, political science, religion,
sociology, and other related subjects. The index is
arranged alphabetically with author and subject entries.
Among the useful subject headings are Richard Milhous Nixon,
United States--History, United States--Politics and
Government, and Presidents--United States.

Social Sciences Citation Index (SSCI). Philadelphia, PA:
     Institute for Scientific Information, 1973-   ;
     quarterly.

Providing access to recent literature in the social and
behavioral sciences, Social Sciences Citation Index reviews
a number of journals and books published worldwide. There

are four parts to the index: a citation index arranged by
author, a corporate index for nonpersonal cited authors
including their geographical location and important
affiliations, a source index that lists who cited whom
where, and a subject index. Useful citations for Richard
Nixon can be found in the subject index by using the term
Nixon.

Social Sciences Index. New York, NY: H.W. Wilson Company,
    1974-   ; quarterly.

Covering the major periodicals in the social sciences,
this index provides a subject and author access to important
articles in anthropology, economics, geography law, public
administration, and criminal justice. A book review section
is also provided. Useful subject headings include Richard
M. Nixon, United States--History, United States--Politics
and Government, and Presidents--United States

Other Abstracts and Indexes

        Criminal Justice Abstracts
        Historical Abstracts
        International Bibliography of Political Science
        Psychological Abstracts
        Sociological Abstracts
        Vance Public Administration Series
        Vertical File Index

Periodicals

Research into the political career of Richard Nixon is
complicated by the numerous "news of the day" articles
written to describe the events in which Nixon was directly
or indirectly involved. Some articles are scholarly and
interpretive. Others are merely narrative in nature. Added
to this body of "news" literature is that dealing with
political commentary or analysis that is also needed by the
researcher in order to access the impact, influence, or
meaning of the varied events, actions, and comments that
comprise the twenty-five year political history of Richard
Nixon. The following annotated list of periodicals is
representative of the many that relate to American politics.

American Journal of Political Science. Austin, TX: Midwest
     Political Science Association, 1957-   ; quarterly.

     Official publication of the Midwest Political Science
Association, the journal publishes articles written by its
members. American government and politics are the primary
interest. Each issue contains about eight articles.

American Political Science Review. Washington, DC:
     American Political Science Association, 1906-   ;
     quarterly.

     This is the journal of the major professional
organization of the political science discipline, American

Political Science Association. Articles are concerned with
American politics, international relations, political
theory, comparative politics, and political methodology.
There are about twelve articles in each issue.

Annals. American Academy of Political and Social Science.
        Philadelphia, PA: American Academy of Political and
        Social Science, 1891-   ; bimonthly.

Published to promote progress in the political and
social sciences, the Annals contains eight to twelve
articles relating to a single theme in each issue. Topics
are diverse with welfare state, insanity defense, and arms
negotiations being among recent topics.

Current History. Philadelphia, PA: Current History,
        1914-   ; monthly.

This is a journal for international affairs study.
Each issue is devoted to one area or country with eight
articles presented. Both news and scholarly comments are
offered on the topics covered.

Foreign Affairs. New York, NY: Council on Foreign
        Relations, 1922-   ; 5 times a year.

As the official publication of the Council on Foreign
Relations, this journal seeks to influence the shaping of
U.S. foreign policy. Each issue contains about ten articles
covering foreign policy issues. There is a book review
section.

Journal of American History. Bloomington, IN: Organization
    of American Historians, 1914-   ; quarterly.

This journal's exclusive concern is American history.
It is the official publication of the Organization of
American Historians. Book reviews, dissertations, and
published bibliographies are included.

Journal of Politics. Gainesville, FL: Southern Political
    Science Association, 1939-   ; quarterly.

The journal is the official publication of the
Political Science Association. It covers primarily American
government and politics. Each issue contains approximately
eight articles. Most of the articles are based upon some
statistical analysis.

Political Science Quarterly. New York, NY: Academy of
    Political Science, 1886-   ; quarterly.

A non-partisan journal devoted to the study of
contemporary and historical aspects of government and
politics. Emphasis is upon American politics with each
issue containing about eight articles.

Presidential Studies Quarterly. New York, NY: Center for
    the Study of the Presidency, 1974-   ; quarterly.

The Center for the Study of the Presidency examines
domestic and foreign policy of presidents. Each issue of
its journal contains about fifteen articles on all aspects

of the American presidency. A book review section is
included.

Western Political Quarterly. Salt Lake City, UT: Western
    Political Science Association, 1948-   ; quarterly.

A general journal of political science, this journal
serves as the official publication of the Western Political
Science Association. Approximately ten articles appear in
each issue. American politics, international politics,
political theory, and public policy are the subjects
emphasized.

Other Periodicals of Interest

    American Political Quarterly

    Atlantic Community Quarterly

    Cato Journal

    Congress and the Presidency

    Foreign Policy

    International Affairs

    International Studies Quarterly

    Journal of International Affairs

    Journal of Policy Analysis and Management

    Journal of Social, Political, and Economic Studies

    Orbis

    PS

    Policy Review

Policy Sciences

Policy Studies Journal

Policy Studies Review

Political Behavior

Political Methodology

Political Quarterly

Political Studies

Political Theory

Politics and Society

Polity

Publius

Review of Politics

Washington Quarterly

World Affairs

World Policy Journal

World Politics

World Today

Biographical Materials

Numerous popular and scholarly works have been written
about Richard Milhous Nixon during the past several decades.
Current Biography considered Nixon significant as early as
1947. Phillip Andrews wrote the first biographical study of
Nixon in 1952, This Man Nixon: The Life Story of California
Senator Richard M. Nixon. Following Nixon's selection as
the Republican nominee for vice-president in 1952, a number
of biographical pieces appeared in print including Ernest
Brashear's "Who Is Richard Nixon?" in the New Republic.
From the early 1950s, Nixon has been a personality with
appeal for authors espousing a political philosophy and
analysts who have tried to categorize Nixon's political
fortunes.

Among the standard biographies are those written by
Ralph DeToledano, Nixon (1956) and One Man Alone (1969).
DeToledano's works are authoritative and serve as the
official record of the events of Nixon's life and political
career up to his election as president, but DeToledano is
also biased in favor of his subject. He indulges in a hero
worship that has become tarnished with the events of the
Watergate scandal. Nixon is the astute politician who is
second to none in serving his country and its democratic
ideals if DeToledano's work is read in ignorance of the

events following the 1972 presidential election campaign.

Countering the hero image so evident in DeToledano's
work are a host of unfavorable treatments written to
discredit and embarrass Nixon when he offered himself as a
candidate for public office. In 1955, the New Statesman
published an article entitled "Synthetic Hero." The New
Republic succeeded in raising doubts about Richard Nixon's
political career by publishing an article entitled the "New
Nixon" in 1958. Arthur Schlesinger, Jr., successfully used
the psychoanalytic approach to discredit Nixon in his work
Kennedy or Nixon (1960), which was written to save the
nation from Nixon's election to the presidency in 1960. In
a rather uncharacteristically subjective work, Schlesinger
summed up his view of Nixon with the statement, "Nixon has
no taste." But the tide of unfavorable works concerning the
life and career of Richard Nixon did acquire a more
scholarly foundation from the publication of Earl Mazo's
Richard Nixon: A Political and Personal Portrait in 1959.
Mazo's book was intended to serve as an objective narrative
of Nixon's life and career. It, thus, inevitably uncovered
the man's warts and family skeletons. Examples of Nixon's
amorality were easily found in Mazo's work. For many
readers and critics, Mazo's work successfully documented
Nixon as a man without principles or conviction.

Following Nixon's election to the presidency in 1968, a

number of works appeared to explain his personality, decisions as president, and controversial policies through the medium of the biography. Gary Allen wrote <u>Richard Nixon: The Man Behind the Mask</u> in 1971. Michael Rogin and John Lottier co-authored an article in <u>Transaction</u> in 1971 entitled "The Inner History of Richard Milhous Nixon." <u>The Nixon Nobody Knows</u> by Henry Spalding was published in 1972. But, the real dramatic change in the Nixon biographical literature occurred following the Watergate scandal and Nixon's subsequent resignation of the presidency. Psychohistory was elevated to an art in forming discriptions and explanations for Richard Nixon, the man who gave up the presidency of the United States. <u>In Search of Nixon: A Psychohistorical Inquiry</u> by Bruce Mazlish was published in 1972. <u>Nixon vs. Nixon: A Psychological Inquest</u> by David Abrahamsen appeared in 1976. James Barber revealed Nixon had a split personality in his article in <u>Psychology Today</u> in 1974, which was entitled "President Nixon and Richard Nixon: A Character Trap." In fact, the continued appearance of psychoanalytic biography pieces concerning Richard Nixon prompted some scholars to question the effectiveness of psychoanalytic studies with regard to Nixon. In 1979, the <u>Chronicle of Higher Education</u> noted the numerous published psychohistories about Nixon in an article entitled "Putting Nixon on the Couch." James Johnson's article "Nixon and the Psychohistorians" published in the

Psychohistory Review cast a shadow over the then-popular
practice of psychoanalyzing Richard Nixon's life.

In 1981, this psychoanalytic characteristic of the
literature written about Richard Nixon reached its zenith
with the publication of Fawn Brodie's Richard Nixon: The
Shaping of His Character, 1913-1963. Brodie's work attempts
to explain the events of Richard Nixon's life and political
career through Freudian analysis. Flaws noted in Nixon's
character, according to Brodie, are directly attributed to
parental influences. For Brodie, Nixon is a man who could
not compensate for the missing parental love in his life
through means other than escaping to fantasy and ultimately
to self-destruction. Glory and power, as Brodie writes,
became the substitute for parental love in Nixon's life and
also the most powerful motivating forces in him.

However, by 1980 Richard Nixon had already assumed a
new stature through comparison with the repudiated
presidency of Jimmy Carter and the jingoistic foreign policy
pursued by the Reagan presidency. Nixon nostalgia appeared
in academic circles. In 1984, Robert Anson published Nixon:
The Unquiet Oblivion of Richard M. Nixon, which objectively
recorded the events of Nixon's life from his resignation of
the presidency in August of 1974 to January of 1983.
Anson's work, though not offering explanations for the
change in Nixon's image, does record the events which have

brought Nixon a new respect and evident esteem among the
American scholarly community and populace. Nixon's travels
to meet with world leaders, Nixon's books on foreign policy,
Nixon's assistance in negotiating an end to the baseball
strike in 1985, and Nixon's advice on foreign policy being
sought by both presidents Carter and Reagan are all in
Anson's work. In 1982, Clifford Griffin's article "The
Magic of Richard Nixon," appeared in American History.
Griffin attempted to explain Nixon's continuing influence on
the American public and thereby confirmed the new stature
that Nixon has gained. These works have brought a new
viewpoint to the Nixon literature, namely that of the
durable public figure whose life is full of the intriguing
contradictions of which good stories are written.

At the same time that some authors are reassessing the
importance of Nixon's life, others are reassessing the Nixon
presidency without the Watergate scandal as a guide. In
1987, Stephen Ambrose published Nixon: The Education of a
Politician, 1913-1962. This work is an objective
examination of the voluminous materials available on Richard
Nixon, the man and the politician. Ambrose sums up his
effort at assessing Nixon's role in American history by
stating "Nixon reminds me of the opening lines of A Tale of
Two Cities. He was the best of presidents; he was the worst
of presidents." The record of Richard Nixon's life is a
series of highs and lows. Even with the events of the early

1970s casting such a hugh shadow, the biographical
literature concerned with Nixon is also now a series of high
and low assessments. As Stephan Ambrose writes "All our
presidents start to look better after we've lived with their
successors, and we have reached a point where you hear
increasingly of nostalgia for Nixon."

1. Abrahamsen, David. *Nixon vs. Nixon: A Psychological
    Inquest*. New York, NY: Farrar, Straus, and
    Giroux, 1976.

2. Adler, Bill. *Wit and Humor of Richard Nixon*. New
    York, NY: Popular Library, 1969.

3. Albert, Ben. "The Political Lives of Richard
    Nixon." *American Federationist* 75 (September
    1986): 1-4.

4. Allen, Gary. *Richard Nixon: The Man Behind the
    Mask*. Boston, MA: Western Island Press,
    1971.

5. Alsop, Stewart. "Mystery of Richard Nixon."
    Saturday Evening Post 231 (July 12, 1958): 28-
    29.

6. _____. *Nixon and Rockefeller*. New York, NY:
    Doubleday, 1960.

7. _____. "Nixon on Nixon." *Saturday Evening Post*
    (July 12, 1958): 26-27.

8. _____. "Richard Nixon: The Mystery and the
    Man." *Readers Digest* 73 (November 1958): 51-
    56.

9. Ambrose, Stephen E. *Nixon: The Education of a
    Politician, 1913-1962*. New York, NY: Simon
    and Schuster, 1987.

10. Anderson, William W. "Self-actualization of
    Richard M. Nixon." Journal of Humanistic
    Psychology 15 (Winter 1975): 27-35.

11. Andrews, Phillip. This Man Nixon: The Life Story
    of California Senator Richard M. Nixon.
    Philadelphia, PA: Winston, 1952.

12. Anson, Robert S. Exile: the Unquiet Oblivion of
    Richard M. Nixon. New York, NY: Simon and
    Schuster, 1984.

13. Deleted.

14. Deleted.

15. Bailey, Thomas A. Presidential Saints and Sinners.
    New York, NY: Free Press, 1981. pp. 260-270.

16. Barber, James D. "President Nixon and Richard
    Nixon: A Character Trap." Psychology Today
    81 (October 1974): 113-114+.

17. _____. Presidential Character: Predicting
    Performance in the White House. Englewood
    Cliffs, NJ: Prentice-Hall, 1972. pp. 345-
    442.

18. Baudhuin, E. Scott. "From Campaign to Watergate:
    Nixon's Communication Image." Western Speech
    38 (Summer 1974): 182-189.

19. Baumgold, Julie. "Nixon's New Life in New York."
    New York 13 (June 9, 1980): 22-25+.

20. "Birth of a Salesman." Our Times New York, NY:
    Farrar and Strauss, 1960. pp. 221-231.

21. Blankenburg, William B. "Nixon vs. the Networks:
    Madison Avenue and Wall Street." Journal of
    Broadcasting 21 (Spring 1977): 163-175.

22. Block, Herbert. Herblock Special Report: Words
    and Pictures on Nixon's Career from Freshman
    Congressman to Full, Free and Absolute Pardon.
    New York, NY: W.W. Norton, 1976.

23. Bonnell, John Sutherland. "Richard Milhous Nixon."
    Presidential Profiles. John S. Bonnell.
    Philadelphia,

24. Bourne, Tom. "In Search of Nixon." Horizon 24
    (February 1981): 42-45.

25. Brashear, Ernest. "Who Is Richard Nixon?" New Republic 127 (September 8, 1952): 9-11.

26. Bremer, Howard F. Richard M. Nixon, 1913- chronology, documents, bibliographic aids. New York, NY: Oceana, 1975.

27. Brodie, Fawn M. Richard Nixon: the Shaping of His Character, 1913-1963. New York, NY: Norton, 1981.

28. Campbell, Ann Raymond. The Picture Life of Richard Milhous Nixon. New York, NY: F. Watts, 1969.

29. Cathcart, Robert S., and Edward A. Schwartz. "New Nixon or Poor Richard." North American Review (US) (September 1968): 8-12.

30. Cavan, Sherri. Twentieth Century Gothic: America's Nixon. San Francisco, CA: Wigan Pier Press, 1979.

31. Cesarini, Sforza, Marco. Nixon. Milan, Italy: Longanesi, 1968.

32. Chesen, Eli, S. President Nixon's Psychiatric Profile (a psychodynamic genetic interpretation). New York, NY: Wyden, 1973.

33. Collins, Frederic William. "Presenting the 1960 Nixon." Nation 185 (November 23, 1957): 381-382.

34. Collins, Robert M. "Richard M. Nixon: The Psychic, Political, and Moral Uses of Sport." Journal of Sport History 10, (Summer 1983): 77-84.

35. Costello, William. Facts About Nixon: An Unauthorized Biography. New York, NY: Viking, 1960.

36. _____. Facts About Nixon: The Unauthorized Biography of Richard M. Nixon, the Formative Years 1913-1959. New York, NY: Viking, 1974.

37. Coughlin, Ellen K. "Putting Richard Nixon on the Couch." Chronicle of Higher Education 17 (February 13, 1979): 3-4.

38. Culbert, David H. "Television's Nixon: The Politician and His Image." American History/American Television. John E. O'Connor. New York, NY: Ungar, 1983, pp. 184-207.

39. "A Decade After His Downfall, A Resurgent Richard Nixon Still Stirs Mixed Emotions and Memories." People Weekly 22 (August 13, 1984): 53-54+.

40. DeToledano, Ralph. Nixon. New York, NY: Holt, Rinehart, Winston, 1956.

41. _____. "Nixon, The Man and His Politics." American Mercury 88 (May 1959): 5-16.

42. _____. One Man Alone: Richard Nixon. New York, NY: Funk and Wagnalls, 1969.

43. Diamond, Edwin. "Psychojournalism: Nixon on the Couch." Columbia Journalism Reviews 7 (March/April 1974): 7-11.

44. "Ex-President Nixon." Commonweal 100 (August 23, 1974): 443-444.

45. Fox, Frank, and Stephen Parker. "Why Nixon Did Himself in: A Behavioral Examination of His Need to Fail." New York Magazine (September 1974): 26-32.

46. Frost, David. I Gave Them a Sword: Behind the Scenes of the Nixon Interviews. New York, NY: Morrow, 1978.

47. Gibson, James W., and Patricia M. Felkins. "A Nixon Lexicon." Western Speeches 38 (Summer 1974): 190-198.

48. Griffin, Clifford S. "The Magic of Richard Nixon." American History 10, 2 (1982): 269-274.

49. Glass, Andrew J. "How Nixon Works." New Leader 57 (March 4, 1974): 4-5.

50. Goldman, Paul, et al. "New Nixon Works." New Leader 57 (March 4, 1974): 4-5.

51. _____. "Nixon's New Life." Newsweek 86 (October 20, 1975): 21-24+.

34

52. Hall, Perry D. Quotable Richard M. Nixon.
    Anderson, SC: Drokehouse, 1967.

53. Halterman, William H. Nixon in Retrospect, 1946-
    1962. New York, NY: Research Data
    Publications, 1973.

54. Hamilton, James W. "Some Reflections on Richard
    Nixon in the Light of His Resignation and
    Farewell Speeches." Journal of Psychohistory
    4 (Spring 1977): 491-511.

55. Harris, Irving D. "The Psychologies of
    Presidents." History of Childhood Quarterly 3
    (Winter 1976): 337-350.

56. Harris, Mark. Mark the Glove Boy or the Last Days
    of Richard Nixon. New York, NY: Macmillan,
    1964.

57. Harrison, Selig S. "Nixon, the Old Guard: Young
    Pretender." New Republic 135 (August 20,
    1956): 9-15.

58. Hart, Roderick P. "Absolutism and Situation:
    Prolegomena to a Rhetorical Biography of
    Richard M. Nixon." Communication Monographs
    43 (August 1976): 204-228.

59. Harwood, Michael. "Richard Nixon." Shadow of
    Presidents. Boston, MA: Lippincott, 1966.
    pp. 200-206.

60. Henderson, Charles P. The Nixon Theology. New
    York, NY: Harper and Row, 1972.

61. Henderson, John T., and Amnon Till. "Leadership
    Personality and War: The Cases of Richard
    Nixon and Anthony Eden." Political Science 28
    (December 1976): 141-171.

62. Heywood, Robert T. President Nixon: The First
    Family Estate: San Clemente, California 1925-
    1969. Laguna, CA: Crown Valley Publishers,
    1970.

63. Higgins, George V. "Friends of Richard Nixon."
    Atlantic 234 (November 1974): 41-52.

64. Hoffman, Paul. The New Nixon. New York, NY:
    Tower Publications, 1970.

65. Holeman, Frank. "Curious Quaker." Candidates
    1960. New York, NY: Basic Books, 1959. pp.
    103-142.

66. Howe, Irving. "Melting Down the Plastic Man."
    Dissent 21 (Summer 1974): 365-366.

67. Hoyt, Edwin P. The Nixons: An American Family.
    New York, NY: Random House, 1972.

68. Hughes, Arthur J. Richard M. Nixon. New York, NY:
    Dodd, Mead, 1972.

69. Hutschnecker, Arnold A. The Drive for Power. New
    York, NY: M. Evans, 1974.

70. Jackson, Donald. "The Young Nixon." Life 68
    (November 6, 1970): 54.

71. Johnson, George. Richard Nixon: An Intimate and Revealing
    Portrait of One of America's Key Political Figures.
    Durby, CT: Monarch Books, 1961.

72. Johnson, James P. "Nixon and the
    Psychohistorians." Psychohistory Review 7, 3
    (1979): 38-42.

73. Kane, Joseph N. "Richard Milhous Nixon." Facts
    About the Presidents: A Compilation of
    Biographical and Historical Data. Joseph N.
    Kane. New York, NY: Ace Books, 1976. pp.
    271-281.

74. Karl, Barry D. "The Nixon Fault." American
    History 7, 2 (1979): 143-156.

75. Karsh, William. "Richard M. Nixon." Illustrated
    London News 229 (November 3, 1956): 761.

76. Kempton, Murray. "Nixon Years--an Obituary."
    Spectator 209 (November 16, 1962): 745.

77. Keogh, James. This Is Nixon. New York, NY:
    Putnam, 1956.

78. "Kicking Nixon Around the Couch." Time 109 (April
    18, 1977): 29-30.

79. King, Robert L. "Transforming Scandal into Tragedy: A Rhetoric of Political Apology." Quarterly Journal of Speech 71 (August 1985): 289-301.

80. Kolson, Katherine L. "Indecent Exposure: Richard Nixon in Exile." Texas Quarterly 19 (Winter 1976): 157-164.

81. Koppman, Lionel, and Bernard Postal. Guess Who's Jewish in American History. New York, NY: Steimatzky/Shapolsky Books, 1986.

82. Kornitzer, Bela. Real Nixon: An Intimate Biography. New York, NY: Rand-McNally, 1960.

83. Lawton, Henry W. "Milhous Rising." Journal of Psychohistory 6 (Spring 1979): 519-542.

84. Liebert, R. S. "Nixon and the Enemy Within." Psychology Today 10 (March 1977): 68-69.

85. "Little Tricky Dick, Views of James W. Hamilton." American Behavior 7 (February 1978): 37.

86. Longford, Frank Pakenham. Nixon: A Study in Extremes of Fortune. London, UK: Weidenfeld and Nicolson, 1980.

87. Marcell, David W. "Poor Richard: Nixon and the Problem of Innocence." American Character and Culture in a Changing World. John Hague, ed. Westport, CT. Greenwood Press, 1979, pp. 325-337.

88. Mankiewicz, Frank. Perfectly Clear: Nixon from Whittier to Watergate. New York, NY: Harper and Row, 1973.

89. Mazlish, Bruce. In Search of Nixon: A Psychohistorical Inquiry. New York, NY: Basic Books, 1972.

90. _____. "Towards a Psychohistorical Inquiry: The Real Richard Nixon." Journal of Interdisciplinary History 1 (Autumn 1970): 49-105.

91. Mazo, Earl. Richard Nixon: A Political and Personal Portrait. New York, NY: Harper and Row, 1959.

92. Mazo, Earl, and Stephen Hess. Nixon, a Political Portrait. New York, NY: Harper and Row, 1968.

93. Mazon, Mauricio. "Young Richard Nixon: A Study in Political Precocity." Historian 41 (November 1978): 21-40.

94. Millen, William Arthur. Nixonia. Fact, Fable, Fantasy. New York, NY: Exposition Press, 1970.

95. Miller, William Lee. "American Failure Story." Commonweal 100 (September 6, 1974: 476-478.

96. _____. "Debating Career of Richard M. Nixon." Reporter 14 (April 19, 1956): 11-17.

97. Monaghan, Frank. Poor Richard's Paradox: A Behavioral Analysis of Richard M. Nixon. Fort Worth, TX: Alpha Publishing Company, 1974.

98. Nathans, Sydney. "Unpardonable Folly." South Atlantic Quarterly 81 (Winter 1982): 6-13.

99. Nuechterlein, James A. "Richard Nixon's Character and Fate." Queen's Quarterly 86 (Spring 1979): 16-25.

100. "New Nixon." New Republic 139 (September 22, 1958): 6.

101. Nixon, Hannah M. "Richard Nixon, A Mother's Story." Good Housekeeping 150 (June 1960): 54-57+.

102. "Nixon: The Lust for Glory." New Statesman 97 (June 22, 1979): 910-912.

103. "Nixon." Current Biography 8 (February 1947): 28-30

104. Osborne, John. "Summing up of a Nixon Watcher." New Republic 159 (October 26, 1968): 15-17.

105. _____. "Was Nixon Sick of Mind?" New York 8 (April 21, 1975): 37-45.

106. Perry, Enos, J. "Richard M. Nixon." Boyhood Days of Our Presidents. Enos J. Perry. Chicago, IL: Adams Press, 1971, pp. 301-307.

107. Potter, Philip. "Political Pitchman." Candidates 1960 New York, NY: Basic Books, 1959. pp. 69-102.

108. Ravenal, Earl C. "Nixon's Challenge to Carter." Foreign Policy 29 (Winter 1977-1978): 27-42.

109. Reichley, A. James. "The Real Richard Nixon Stands
        Up." Fortune 87 (April 1973): 53-57.

110. Reshon, Stanley A. "Psychological Analysis and
        Presidential Personality: The Case of Richard
        Nixon." History of Childhood Quarterly 2 (Winter
        1975): 415-450.

111. "Return of the Native." Time 77 (March 10, 1961):
        20.

112. "Richard Nixon." Book of Presidents. Tim Taylor.
        New York, NY: Arno Press, 1972. pp. 581-634.

113. "Richard M. Nixon." Glorious Burden. Stefan Lorant.
        Lenox, MA: Authurs, 1976. pp. 905-1011.

114. "Richard Nixon." Madmen and Geniuses. Sol Barzman.
        Chicago, IL: Follett, 1974. pp. 253-260.

115. "Richard M. Nixon." My Eight Presidents. Sarah
        McClendon. New York, NY: Wyden Books, 1978. pp.
        162-180.

116. "Richard M. Nixon." Current Biography 9 (July 1948):
        36-37.

117. "Richard M. Nixon." Fortune 41 (March 1980): 67.

118. "Richard M. Nixon." Life 29 (August 28, 1950): 104.

119. "Richard M. Nixon." Time 68 (November 5, 1956): 28.

120. "Richard M. Nixon." Current Biography 19 (June 1958):
        25-27.

121. "Richard Nixon." Current Biography 30 (December
        1969): 27-30.

122. "Richard M. Nixon." in Vice Presidents and Cabinet
        Members. Vol. II. Robert I. Vexler. New York,
        NY: Oceana, 1975. pp. 666-669.

123. "Richard M. Nixon." in Political Profiles: the
        Nixon/Ford Years. Eleanor W. Schoenebaum. New
        York, NY: Facts on File, 1979. pp. 466-479.

124. "Richard M. Nixon--The Early Years: His Case Brought
        National Prominence." Biography News 1 (September
        1974): 1065-1070.

125. "Richard M. Nixon: End of a Remarkable Career."
      Congressional Quarterly Weekly Reports 32 (August
      10, 1974): 2083-2091.

126. "Richard Nixon's Story--A Tumultuous Career." US News
      and World Report 77 (August 19, 1974): 33-36.

127. Robinson, David. "Nixon in Crisis-Land: The Rhetoric
      of Six Crises." Journal of American Culture 8
      (Spring 1985): 79-85.

128. Rogin, Michael, and John Lottier. "The Inner History
      of Richard Milhous Nixon." Transaction 9
      (November/December 1971): 19-28.

129. Rosenfield, Laurence W. "A Case Study in Speech
      Criticism: the Nixon-Truman Analog." Speech
      Monographs 35, (November 1968): 435-460.

130. Rothenberg, Alan B. "Why Nixon Taped Himself."
      Psychoanalytic Review 62 (Summer 1975): 201-233.

131. Rovere, Robert H. "Three Nixons." Spectator 201
      (November 7, 1958): 600.

132. Schiff, Lawrence F. "Dynamic Young Fogies--Rebels on
      the Right." Transaction 4 (November/December
      1966): 32-39.

133. Schlesinger, Arthur M., Jr. Kennedy or Nixon. New
      York, NY: Macmillan, 1960.

134. Schnapper, Morris B. Quotations from the Would-Be
      Chairman: Richard Milhous Nixon. Washington, DC:
      Public Affairs Press, 1968.

135. Schulte, Renee K. Young Nixon: an Oral Inquiry.
      Fullerton, CA: California State University, 1978.

136. Seelye, John. "Measure of His Company: Richard Nixon
      in Amber." Virginia Quarterly Review 53 (Autumn
      1977): 585-606.

137. Shaffer, Samuel. "Nixon: What Next?" Newsweek 82
      (November 12, 1973): 24-27+

138. Shawcross, William. "Fortunes of Richard Nixon." New
      Statesman 86 (October 19, 1973): 544-545.

139. Spalding, Henry D. The Nixon Nobody Knows. Middle
     Village, NY: Jonathan David, 1972.

140. Steinfield, Melvin. Our Racist Presidents from
     Washington to Nixon. San Ramon, CA: Consensus
     Publishers, 1972.

141. Stone, Irving. "Richard Nixon." They Also Ran.
     Irving Stone. New York, NY: Doubleday, 1966.
     pp. 406.

142. Storer, Doug. "Richard Milhous Nixon." Amazing but
     True: Stories About the Presidents. Doug Storer.
     New York, NY: Pocket Books, 1975. pp. 190-193.

143. Swayduck, Edward. "Sabotage: Since 1946, Nixon's
     Political Stock-in-Trade." Lithopinion 8 (Summer
     1973): 2-7.

144. "Synthetic Hero." New Statesman 49 (January 22, 1955):
     100-101.

145. "That New, New Nixon." Economist 248 (August 18,
     1973): 13-14.

146. "Two Decades of Crisis Between Nixon and the Media."
     Broadcasting 87 (August 19, 1974): 22-23.

147. Voorhis, Horace Jermiah. The Strange Case of Richard
     Milhous Nixon. New York, NY: Popular Library,
     1973.

148. West, Jessamyn. "Jessamyn West Talks About Her Cousin
     President Nixon." McCalls 96.

149. Westin, Ablan F., and John Stattuck. "The Second
     Deposing of Richard Nixon." Civil Liberties
     Review 3 (June/July 1976): 8-23; 84-96.

150. White, William Smith. "Nixon: What Kind of
     President?" Harper 216 (January 1958): 25-30.

151. Whitfield, Stephen J. "Richard Nixon as a Comic
     Figure." American Quarterly 37 (Spring 1985):
     114-132.

152. Whitney, David C. "Richard Milhous Nixon." American
     Presidents. David C. Whitney. New York, NY:
     Doubleday, 1978. pp. 347-382.

153. "Who Is Nixon, What Is He?" Our Times New York, NY: Farrar and Straus, 1960. pp. 232-240.

154. Wicker, Tom. "Nixon Starts over Alone." New York Times Magazine (May 16, 1962): 17.

155. Wills, Garry. Nixon Agonistes. Boston, MA: Houghton Mifflin, 1970.

156. Wilson, Richard. "Big Change in Richard Nixon." Look 21 (September 3, 1957): 66-69.

157. _____. "Is Nixon Fit to Be President?" Look 17 (February 24, 1953): 33-42.

158. Witcover, Jules. The Resurrection of Richard Nixon. New York, NY: G.P. Putnam's Sons, 1970.

159. _____. "Richard M. Nixon: The Man Nobody Knows." Progressive 33 (January 1969): 13-16.

160. Woodstone, Arthur. Nixon's Head. New York, NY: St. Martin's Press, 1972.

161. _____. The Head of Richard Nixon. New York, NY: Popular Library, 1976.

162. Young, Donald. "Richard M. Nixon." American Roulette. Donald Young. New York, NY: Holt, Rinehart, Winston, 1965. pp. 252-285.

Alger Hiss

In 1948, at a hearing before the House Un-American
Activities Committee Congressman Richard Nixon, a committee
member, assisted in presenting evidence that implicated
Alger Hiss, a respected member of the Truman administration,
in subversive activities. Alger Hiss was subsequently found
guilty of lying about his espionage activities by a jury of
his peers. The Hiss case put Richard Nixon on the ladder to
the presidency of the United States. However since 1948,
the Hiss case has been fiercely debated. Each of the
principal characters in the case has written his
respective version. Alger Hiss wrote his In the Court of
Public Opionion in 1957 in order to document his innocence.
Whittaker Chambers, a professed former Communist Party member
who provided the House Un-American Activities Committee with
testimony incriminating Alger Hiss, confirmed his testimony
in Witness in 1952. Richard Nixon has related his role in
the Hiss case several times. In 1962, Nixon wrote "The
Strange Case of Alger Hiss" for the Readers' Digest, which
was based upon the account given in his book Six Crises
(1962).

From the beginning of the case in 1948, there has been

considerable sentiment that Alger Hiss was the victim of
partisan politics. Thomas Sancton's article for the Nation
entitled "The Case of Alger Hiss" in September of 1948
strongly concluded that the charges against Hiss were
neither proved nor disproved by the testimony given to the
House Un-American Activities Committee. Walter Millis and
others pondered "Was Alger Hiss Framed?" in a 1958 issue of
the Saturday Evening Post. Questions have been raised about
the Hiss case by numerous works that have examined the near
hysteria of the late 1940s over communist infiltration of
the U.S. government. Ronald Seth's Sleeping Truth (1968)
and Meyer Zelig's Friendship and Fratricide: An Analysis of
Whittaker Chambers and Alger Hiss (1967) both raised more
questions than provided answers about the facts of the Hiss
case. In the 1970s the work of Allen Weinstein, Perjury:
The Hiss-Chambers Case (1979), effectively destroyed the
innocence argument used by Alger Hiss's supporters.
Weinstein, writing a brilliant examination of the available
evidence for the case, concluded that Alger Hiss was guilty
of lying and espionage. Yet, despite Weinstein's work,
there is still no agreement on the issue of Hiss's guilt as
witnessed by the refutation of Weinstein's conclusion in the
Journal of American Studies in 1979 entitled "Review Essay:
Weinstein on Hiss."

Alger Hiss's guilt will obviously be debated for years
to come. Richard Nixon's method and motivation in the

exposure of Hiss's subversive activities have also been debated since the Hiss case was heard. Garry Wills's article written for the New York Times Magazine in 1974, "The Hiss Connection Through Nixon's Life," accurately describes the resurrections of the Hiss case each time Richard Nixon campaigned for public office. In the early years of Nixon's political career, the Hiss case was used by Nixon to smear opponents as communist sympathizers and gain an advantage in a political campaign as occurred in the 1950 U.S. Senate election in California and the 1952 presidential election when Nixon was the Republican Party nominee for vice-president. During those years, Richard Nixon was the champion of the Republic, who courageously exposed the internal danger from communist sympathizers hidden in the federal bureaucracy. But, in subsequent years, the Hiss case became a symbol of Nixon's amoral approach to politics and has been exploited by opponents to embarrass and harrass Nixon. In 1958, William Reuben wrote The Honorable Mr. Nixon and the Alger Hiss Case which serves as a model for such Nixon criticism. Reuben demanded that Nixon, then the leading candidate in the 1960 presidential campaign, be judged by his record in the Alger Hiss case. Reuben insisted that Nixon misled and maneuvered the American public into accepting Hiss's guilt for his personal political gain.

45

163. "Adlai Stevenson and Alger Hiss." Commonweal 56
     (August 22, 1952): 475-476.

164. "Alger Hiss Argues His Innocence." Newsweek 49 (May
     13, 1957): 40+.

165. "Alger Hiss at Princeton." Commonweal 64 (April 27,
     1956): 89. Discussion: Commonweal 64 (June 1,
     1956): 227-228.

166. "Alger Hiss Story." Time 69 (May 13, 1957): 27-28.

167. Altman, George T. "Added Witness." Nation 191
     (October 1, 1960): 201-209.

168. Andrews, Bert, and Peter Andrews. Tragedy of History
     (Journalist's confidential role in the Hiss-
     Chambers case). New York, NY: Luce Books, 1962.

169. Atkins, Ollie. "Pumpkin Papers and a Generation on
     Trial." Saturday Evening Post 248 (January 1976):
     40-41+.

170. Barros, James. "Alger Hiss and Harry Dexter White:
     The Canadian Connection." Orbis 21 (Fall 1977):
     593-605.

171. Begeman, Jean. "Hiss and Stevenson--The Truth." New
     Republic 127 (August 25, 1952): 10-12.

172. Bell, James A. "Eight out of 12 Vote Hiss Guilty."
     Life 27 (July 18, 1949): 37-40.

173. Bendiner, Robert. "Ordeal of Alger Hiss." Nation 170
     (February 4, 1950): 100-103.

174. _____. "Trial of Alger Hiss." Nation 168 (June
     11, 1949): 650-651.

175. _____. "Trial of Alger Hiss." Nation 168 (June
     25, 1949): 699-700.

176. _____. "Trial of Alger Hiss." Nation 169 (July
     16, 1949): 52-55.

177. Bingham, Robert and Max Ascoli. "Case of Alger Hiss."
     Our Time. New York, NY: Farrar, Strauss, 1960.
     pp. 153-161.

178. Boulton, Wayne K., and C. Dickerson Williams. "Two
      Experts Examine Alger Hiss's Story." Saturday
      Review 40 (May 18, 1957): 25+.

179. Brodie, Fawn M. "I Think Hiss Is Lying." American
      Heritage 32 (August/September 1980): 4-21.

180. Bush, Frances X. Guilty or Not Guilty. New York, NY:
      Bobbs, Merrill, 1952. pp. 197-287.

181. Carr, Robert K. The House Committee on Un-American
      Activities, 1945-1950. Ithaca, NY: Cornell
      University Press, 1952.

182. "Case of Alger Hiss." Time 55 (February 13, 1950):
      22-23.

183. Chambers, Whittaker. "Hissiad, Correction" in
      National Review (1960): 72-73.

184. _____. Witness. New York, NY: Random House,
      1952.

185. Cook, Fred J. "Alger Hiss--A New Ball Game." Nation
      231 (October 11, 1980): 340-343.

186. _____. "Hiss, New Perspectives on the Strangest
      Case of Our Time." Nation 185 (September 21,
      1957): 142-180.

187. _____. "Nixon Kicks a Hole in the Hiss Case."
      Nation 194 (April 7, 1962): 296.

188. _____. Unfinished Story of Alger Hiss. New York,
      NY: Morrow, 1958.

189. Cooke, Alistair. Generation on Trial: USA vs. Alger
      Hiss. New York, NY: Knopf, 1950.

190. Cooney, Thomas E. "Alger Hiss's Story." Saturday
      Review 40 (May 11, 1957): 16+.

191. Costello, William. "Hiss Case." New Republic 141
      (December 7, 1959): 10-16.

192. Countryman, Vern. "One Small Step for Alger Hiss."
      New Republic 173 (August 30, 1975): 14-17.

193. Crossman, Richard Howard Stafford. "Hiss Case."
      Political Quarterly 24 (October 1953): 396-403.

194. "Curiosity at Princeton." Newsweek 47 (April 23, 1956): 60.

195. Dawson, Nelson L. "Unequal Justice: McCarthy and Hiss." Midstream 27, 4 (1981): 13-16.

196. DeToledano, Ralph. "Alger Hiss Story." American Mercury 76 (June 1953); 13-20.

197. DeToledano, Ralph, and Victor Lasky. Seeds of Treason: The True Story of the Hiss-Chambers Tragedy. New York, NY: Funk and Wagnalls, 1950.

198. _____. The Strange Case of Alger Hiss. New York, NY: Secher and Warburg, 1950.

199. Elstein, David. "How They Made Sure Alger Hiss Was Guilty." New Statesman 96 (October 27, 1978): 536-538.

200. "End of the Hiss Case." Time 57 (April 2, 1951): 9.

201. Footlick, John K. "Reviewing the Hiss Case." Newsweek 87 (March 29, 1976): 53.

202. Galbraith, John Kenneth. "Alger Hiss and Liberal Anxiety." Atlantic 241 (May 1978): 44-47.

203. "Ghost of Alger Hiss." New Republic 134 (April 23, 1956): 5.

204. Green, Gil. "Forgery by Typewriter." Nation 239 (November 10, 1984): 468-469.

205. Grossman, James. "Lord Jowitt and the Case of Alger Hiss." Commentary 16 (December 1953): 582-586.

206. Hiss, Alger. The Alger Hiss Case: Basic Documents. New York, NY: Victory Rabnowitz, 1982.

207. _____. In the Court of Public Opinion. New York, NY: Knopf, 1957.

208. Hiss, Tony. Laughing Last: Alger Hiss. Boston, MA: Houghton Mifflin, 1977.

209. "Hiss, A New Book Finds Him Guilty as Charged." Time 111 (February 13, 1978): 28-30.

210. "Hiss Case Ends at Last." Life 30 (April 2, 1951): 32.

211. "Hiss Still Guilty." Newsweek 36 (December 18, 1950):
        32.

212. Hook, Sidney. "An Autobiographical Fragment: The
        Strange Case of Whittaker Chambers." Encounter 46
        (July 1976): 78-89.

213. _____. "The Case of Alger Hiss." Encounter 51
        (August 1978): 48-55.

214. Hudson, Geoffrey Francis. "Lord Jowitt and Hiss
        Trials." Twentieth Century 154 (July 1953):
        20-32.

215. Jeffrey-Jones, Rhodri. "Review Essay: Weinstein on
        Hiss." Journal of American Studies 13 (April
        1979); 115-126.

216. Jowitt, William. Strange Case of Alger Hiss. New
        York, NY: Doubleday, 1953.

217. Kinsley, Michael, and Arthur Lubow. "Alger Hiss and
        the Smoking Gun Fallacy." Washington Monthly 7
        (October 1975): 52-60.

218. Lamparski, Richard. Whatever Became of .... New
        York, NY: Crown Publishers, 1967. pp. 16-17.

219. Lasky, Melvin J. "John Reed and Alger Hiss: Two
        Cases in Ideology." Encounter 59 (August 1982):
        86-93.

220. Ledeen, Michael. "Hiss, Oswald, the KGB and Us."
        Commentary 65 (May 1978): 30-36.

221. Lerner, Max. "Hiss and America's Moral Climate." New
        Statesman and Nation 39 (February 11, 1950): 152-
        153.

222. "Lesson of the Hiss Case." Saturday Evening Post 258
        (April 1986): 55-56+.

223. Levin, David. "In the Court of Historical Criticism:
        Alger Hiss's Narrative." Virginia Quarterly
        Review 52 (Winter 1976): 41-78.

224. _____. "Perjury, History, and Unreliable
        Witnesses." Virginia Quarterly Review 54 (Winter
        1978): 725-732.

225. Levitt, Morton, and Michael Levitt. Tissue of
     Lies: Nixon vs. Hiss. New York, NY: McGraw-
     Hill, 1979.

226. Liebling, Abbott Joseph. "Spotlight on the Jury."
     New Yorker 25 (July 23, 1949); 60-62+.

227. McColloch, Charles. "Strange Case of Alger Hiss: A
     Reply to Lord Jowitt." American Bar Association
     Journal 40 (March 1954): 199-202+.

228. McWilliams, Carey. "Will Nixon Exonerate Hiss?"
     Nation 221 (September 20, 1975): 229-231.

229. Marburg, William L. "The Hiss-Chambers Libel Suit."
     Maryland History Magazine 76 (March 1981): 70-92.

230. "Meaning of the Hiss Case." Readers' Digest 61
     (November 1952): 55-60.

231. Miller, Merle. "Second Hiss Trial." New Republic 122
     (February 6, 1950): 11-14.

232. Millis, Walter, et al. "Was Alger Hiss Framed? A
     Debate." Saturday Review 41 (May 31, 1958): 14-
     17+.

233. _____. "Quiet Night at the Whig-Clio." Reporter
     14 (May 17, 1956): 22-23.

234. Moore, Thomas. "Alger Hiss Framed? A Debate."
     Saturday Review 41 (May 31, 1958): 14-17+.

235. Morris, Richard B. Fair Trial. New York, NY: Alfred
     Knopf, 1952. pp. 426-478.

236. "Nixon and the Hiss Case." Nation 218 (May 25, 1974):
     644.

237. Nobile, Philip. "State of the Art of Alger Hiss."
     Harper 252 (April 1976); 67-68+.

238. Ratchcliff, Samuel K. "Tragedy of Alger Hiss."
     Fortnightly 173 (March 1950): 168-173.

239. Reuben, William A. Honorable Mr. Nixon and the Alger
     Hiss Case. New York, NY: Action Books, 1956.

240. _____. "New Development." Nation 239 (November
     10, 1984): 469.

241. Rovere, Richard H. "From Hiss to Van Doren."
     Spectator 203 (November 20, 1959): 690-691.

242. Sancton, Thomas. The Case of Alger Hiss."
     Nation 167 (September 4, 1948): 251-252.

243. Seth, Ronald. _Sleeping Truth; The Hiss-Chambers_
     Affair: The Spy Case That Split a Nation.
     New York, NY: Frewin, 1968.

244. Sklar, Robert. "Tolerant Tiger: Alger Hiss at
     Princeton." _Nation_ 182 (May 5, 1956): 374-
     376.

245. "Slander of a Dead Man." _Time_ 99 (February 10,
     1967): 102+.

246. Smith, John Chabot. _Alger Hiss: The True Story_.
     New York, NY: Holt, Rinehart, Winston, 1976.

247. Stripling, Robert E. _Red Plot Against America_.
     New York, NY: Bell Publishing Company, 1949.

248. Strout, Robert. "Trial of Alger Hiss." _New_
     Statesman and Nation 38 (July 16, 1949): 65-
     66.

249. Theoharis, Athan G. _Beyond the Hiss Case: the_
     FBI, Congress and the Cold War. Philadelphia,
     PA: Temple University Press, 1982.

250. Tiger, Edith. _In re Alger Hiss: Petition from_
     Writ of Error Coram Nobis. New York, NY:
     Hill and Wang, 1979.

251. Trilling, Diana. "Memorandum on the Hiss Case."
     Partisan Review 17 (May 1950): 484-500.

252. "Two Men." _Time_ 52 (December 20, 1948): 17-21.

253. VanDusen, George. "The Continuing Hiss:
     Whittaker Chambers, Alger Hiss and National
     Review Conservatism." _Cithara_ 11, 1 (1971):
     67-89.

254. "Verdict: Hiss Has Been Lying." _Time_ 107 (March
     29, 1976): 30-31.

255. Viereck, Peter R. "Symbols: Hiss and Pound."
     Commonweal 55 (March 28, 1952): 607-608.

256. Weinstein, Allen. "The Alger Hiss Case
     Revisited." American Scholar 41 (Winter
     1972): 121-132.

257. _____. "Nixon on Hiss." Esquire 84 (November
     1975): 73-80+.

258. _____. Perjury: The Hiss-Chambers Case. New
     York, NY: Alfred Knopf, 1976.

259. Wills, Garry. "Hiss Connection Through Nixon's
     Life." New York Times Magazine (August 25,
     1974): 8+.

260. _____. "Honor of Alger Hiss." New York Review
     of Books 25 (April 10, 1978): 29-30.

261. Wittner, Felix. "Literary Debut of Alger Hiss."
     American Mercury 82 (February 1956): 134-140.

262. Younger, Irving. "Was Alger Hiss Guilty?"
     Commentary 60 (August 1975): 23-37.

263. Zeligs, Meyer A. Friendship and Fratricide: An
     Analysis of Whittaker Chambers and Alger Hiss.
     New York, NY: Viking, 1967.

Political Campaigns

William Reuben, in his work The Honorable Mr. Nixon and the Alger Hiss Case (1956), granted Richard Nixon one undisputed area of expertise, that of political campaigner. This praise from another vehement critic was a natural conclusion based upon the devastatingly effective campaigns Richard Nixon waged for the U.S. House in 1946 and the U.S. Senate in 1950. The 1946 U.S. House campaign in southern California between Richard Nixon and Jerry Voorhis is well documented by Paul Bullock. In 1973, Bullock wrote "Rabbits and Radicals: Richard Nixon's 1946 Campaign Against Jerry Voorhis," for the Southern California Quarterly. This work was followed in 1978 by Bullock's Jerry Voorhis: The Idealist as Politician. Ingrid Scobie detailed the 1950 U.S. Senate campaign in California with her article "Helen Gahagan Douglas and Her 1950 Senate race with Richard M. Nixon," written for the Southern California Quarterly in 1976. Both these authors leave little doubt that Nixon was a master campaigner who used all possible tricks to smear his opponents with scandals, doubt, or suspicion in the voters' perception of the individual if not the media as well.

Much has been written about Nixon's campaign tactics. Each political campaign in which Nixon ever engaged ended

with questions and concerns over the methods used by the
Nixon campaign organization. In 1947, the newly elected
congressman, Richard Nixon, was quietly avoided in the halls
of Congress as a means of censoring the tactics used in the
campaign which defeated the popular Jerry Voorhis. In 1973,
the newly re-elected President Richard Nixon encountered the
Senate Select Committee to Investigate the 1972 Presidential
Campaign. The accusation of "dirty tricks" has accompanied
each Nixon campaign for political office. In the 1952
presidential campaign with Richard Nixon as the Republican
Party nominee for vice-president, Nixon was accused of
maintaining a slush fund to cover personal expenses while in
political office. The notorious Checkers speech was
Nixon's reply to his critics. The episode is carefully
reviewed in Arthur Rowse's Slanted News: A Case Study of
the Nixon and Stevenson Fund Stories (1957). Nixon's
manipulation of the media in the 1968 presidential campaign
is well documented in Joe McGinniss's The Selling of the
President 1968 (1969). Watergate and the series of
revelations about the campaign tactics used during the 1972
presidential campaign to discredit serious and imaginary
opponents by the Nixon campaign organization are matters of
public record, having been investigated by the U.S. Senate.
James Judson and Dorothy Lehman have also provided a good
summation of the 1972 campaign tactics in their article
"Lessons of Watergate: The Nixon Campaigns," which appeared

in Current History in 1974.

All these political campaigns have a common feature, namely, efforts to discredit whoever was then the Nixon opponent in a political campaign even before the Nixon candidacy was fully visible or official. Much has been written about the campaign tactics that Nixon employed so frequently by such psychohistorians as Fawn Brodie and Bruce Mazlish. This style of political campaign is best seen in the work of Murray Chotiner, Nixon's political advisor for several decades. Chotiner perfected the campaign technique of finding the opposition's weak points and then keeping media focus upon these very points in California state political races. Chotiner advised both Senator Knowland and Governor Earl Warren in their state campaigns. Richard Nixon hired Chotiner as an advisor for the 1947 congressional campaign and continued the association afterward. From Chotiner, Nixon learned that political victory could be achieved through attacking opponents over remote scandals or associations with unpopular ideas or causes from their early years as students, lawyers, businessmen, or whatever. This is the common thread that connects the Nixon political campaigns from 1947 to 1972. It was successful but destructive of numerous politicians' lives and ultimately undid Nixon's own landslide vindication victory in the 1972 presidential election.

House Campaign

264. Bowers, Lynn and Dorothy Blair. "How to Pick a
      Congressman." Saturday Evening Post 221 (March 19,
      1949): 31+.

265. Bullock, Paul. Jerry Voorhis the Idealist as Politician.
      New York, NY: Vantage Press, 1978.

266. _____. "Rabbits and Radicals: Richard Nixon's 1946
      Campaign Against Jerry Voorhis." Southern California
      Quarterly 55 (Fall 1973): 319-359.

267. Goldman, Eric Frederick. "1947 Kennedy Nixon Tube City
      Debate." Saturday Review 4 (October 16, 1976): 12-13.

268. Richter, Irving. "Congressman Nixon Views Labor Relations,
      1947." Labor History 21 (Spring 1980): 277-278.

Senate Campaign

269. "California Foot Race." Newsweek 35 (June 5, 1950): 25-
      26.

270. DeToledano, Ralph. "Roaring Races." Newsweek 36 (October
      30, 1950): 21.

271. Flannery, Harry W. "Red Smear in California." Commonweal
      53 (December 8, 1950): 225.

272. Moley, Raymond. "Nixon vs Douglas." Newsweek 36 (August
      28, 1950): 84.

273. O'Connor, Collen M. "Imagine the Unimaginable: Helen
      Gahagan Douglas, Women, and the Bomb." Southern
      California Quarterly 67 (Spring 1985): 35-50.

274. Scobie, Ingrid Winther. "Helen Gahagan Douglas and Her
      1950 Senate Race with Richard M. Nixon." Southern
      California Quarterly 58 (Spring 1976): 113-126.

275. "Telling What Happened in the Election." U.S. News and
      World Report 29 (November 17, 1950): 29-30.

1952 Presidential Campaign

276. "Affair Nixon." _Commonweal_ 56 (October 3, 1952): 620.

277. Begeman, Jean. "Nixon: How the Press Suppressed the
      News." _New Republic_ 127 (October 6, 1952): 11-13.

278. Blackburn, Mark. "Another Nixon Angel?" _New Republic_ 127
      (November 3, 1952): 10.

279. Brashear, Ernest. "Who Is Richard Nixon?" _New Republic_
      127 (September 1, 1952): 9-12.

280. "Defense of Checkers." _Commonweal_ 57 (October 10, 1952):
      3.

281. Diamond, Edwin, and Stephen Bates. _The Spot: The Rise of
      Political Advertising on Television_. Cambridge, MA:
      MIT Press, 1984.

282. "Fighting Quaker." _Time_ 60 (August 25, 1952): 13-15.

283. Hartnett, Robert C. "Press Comment on the Nixon Case."
      America 88 (October 11, 1952): 40-41.

284. "Issue of Principle." _Nation_ 175 (October 4, 1952): 287-
      289.

285. McGuckin, Henry E. "A Value Analysis of Richard Nixon's
      1952 Campaign Fund Speech." _Southern Speech Journal_ 33
      (Summer 1968): 259-269.

286. "More on Nixon." _New Republic_ 127 (October 13, 1952): 2.

287. Morris, Joe Alex. "I Say He's a Wonderful Guy." _Readers'
      Digest_ 61 (October 1952): 13-18.

288. "Nixon Affair." _Newsweek_ (October 6, 1952): 23-25.

289. "Nixon Affair: Its Meaning." _U.S. News and World Report_
      33 (October 3, 1952): 18-20.

290. "Nixon Defends Fund." _Scholastic_ 61 (October 1, 1952):
      11.

291. "Nixon Fights, Wins, and Weeps." _Life_ 33 (October 6,
      1952): 25-31.

292. "Nominee for Veep." _Time_ 60 (July 21, 1952): 20.

293. "Record of the Nixon Affair; Legal Opinion, List of
      Contributors, Audit, Speeches, Statements, and
      Documents." U.S. News and World Report 33 (October 3,
      1952): 61-70+.

294. "Remarkable Tornado." Time 60 (September 29, 1952): 11-
      13.

295. "Richard Nixon's Secret Income." New Republic 127
      (September 29, 1952): 10-11+.

296. Rowse, Arthur Edward. Slanted News: A Case Study of the
      Nixon and Stevenson Fund Stories. Boston, MA: Beacon
      Press, 1957.

297. "Who Is Richard Nixon?" New Republic 127 (September 8,
      1952): 36.

298. Why It's Nixon." U.S. News and World Report 33 (July 18,
      1952): 36.

299. Wyatt, William. "If Nixon Lived in Britain." New Republic
      127 (October 6, 1952): 9-10.

1954 Congressional Campaign

300. "Vice President Nixon's Own Story of Campaign." U.S. News
      and World Report 37 (November 12, 1954): 46-49.

1956 Congressional Campaign

301. "Dick Nixon Delivers." Nation 1985 (August 3, 1957): 42.

302. "Did Nixon Hurt the Ticket?" U.S. World and News
      Report 42 (February 8, 1957): 40-42+.

303. "Will Nixon Be on the Ticket Again?" U.S. News and
      World Report 41 (August 10, 1956): 25-28.

1958 Congressional Campaign

304. Boroson, William. "What Makes Nixon Run?" Avant-
      Garde 1 (January 1958): 1-9.

305. Phillips, Charles. "Nixon in '58 and Nixon in '60."
     New York Times Magazine (October 26, 1958): 11+.

1960 Presidential Campaign

306. Alsop, Stewart. "Campaigning with Nixon." Saturday
     Evening Post 233 (November 5, 1960): 32-33+.

307. Altschull, J. Herbert. "The Journalist and Instant
     History: An Example of Jackal Syndrome."
     Journalism Quarterly 50 (Autumn 1973): 489-496.

308. Cater, Douglass. "Unleashing of Richard M. Nixon."
     Reporter 23 (September 1, 1960): 32-34.

309. Costello, William. "Nixon on the Eve, a Candidate in
     Search of an Identity." New Republic (November 7,
     1960): 17.

310. "Debating the Great Debate." Nation 191 (November 5,
     1960): 342-247.

311. Ellsworth, John W. "Rationality and Campaigning: A
     Content Analysis of the 1960 Presidential Campaign
     Debates." Western Political Quarterly 18
     (December 1960): 794-802.

312. Greenfield, Meg. "Prose of Richard M. Nixon."
     Reporter 23 (September 29, 1960): 15-20.

313. "Here's Nixon's Plan to Win in 1960." U.S. News and
     World Report 45 (December 12, 1958): 84-86.

314. Kallina, Edmund F. "The State's Attorney and the
     President: The Inside Story of the 1960
     Presidential Election in Illinois." Journal of
     American Studies 12 (August 1978): 147-160.

315. _____. "Was Nixon Cheated in 1960? Tracing the
     Vote-Fraud Legend." Journalism Quarterly 62
     (Spring 1985): 138-140.

316. _____. "Was the 1960 Presidential Election Stolen:
     The Case of Illinois." Presidential Studies
     Quarterly 15 (Winter 1985): 113-118.

317. Kehl, James A. "Presidential Sweepstakes in Review:
     Seen from the 1960 Starting Gate." Pennsylvania
     Historical Quarterly 31 (1964): 216-228.

318. Karaus, Sidney. The Great Debates: Background,
     Perspectives, Effects. Bloomington, IN: Indiana
     University Press, 1962.

319. Margolis, Howard. "Nixon on Education: His Policy
     Paper Endorses a Broad, Expensive Program of
     Federal Support." Science 132 (September 30,
     1960): 881-883.

320. "Nixon and the Press." Time 76 (August 8, 1960): 50-
     51.

321. "Nixon with Golden Gloves, First Television Debate."
     Nation 191 (October 8, 1960): 218.

322. Pell, Robert. "Foreign Policies of Richard Milhous
     Nixon." America 104 (October 8, 1960): 38-42.

323. "Reviewing the '60 Debates." Time 108 (September 13,
     1976): 12-13.

324. Sevareid, Eric. Candidates 1960: Behind the
     Headlines in the Presidential Race. New York, NY:
     Basic Books, 1960.

325. White, Theodore. The Making of the President, 1960.
     New York, NY: Atheneum, 1961.

1962 California Gubernatorial Campaign

326. "Brassy Fight for a Golden Prize: Nixon vs Brown."
     Life 53 (October 19, 1962): 44-53.

327. Brogan, Denis William. "Problems of Richard Nixon."
     Commentary 34 (September 1962); 261-265.

328. "California: Career's End." Time 80 (April 16,
     1962): 28.

329. "Crisis Number Seven." New Republic 146 (June 18,
     1962): 6.

330. Goulden, Joseph C. "Warming up for Watergate: 1962
     Nixon-Brown California Gubernatorial Election."
     Nation 216 (May 28, 1973): 688-691.

331. Hill, Gladwin. "Do-or-die for Nixon." Saturday
     Evening Post 235 (May 12, 1962): 17-25.

332. McWillams, Carey. "Has Success Spoiled Dick Nixon?"
      Nation 194 (June 2, 1962): 486-493.

333. "Mr. Nixon and the Press." Nation 195 (November 17,
      1962): 486-493.

334. "Nixon Bows Out: Has Last News Conference." U.S.
      News and World Report 53 (November 19, 1962): 19.

335. "Nixon vs Brown: California Is Bigger Prize Now."
      Business Week (June 16, 1962): 16.

336. "Progressive Conservative." Time 79 (June 15, 1962):
      14-15.

337. Steif, William. "Nixon's Uphill Campaign." New
      Republic 146 (February 26, 1962): 18-20.

338. _____. "Richard Nixon on the Knife's Edge." New
      Republic (August 7, 1961): 10.

339. "Tasteless Post-Mortem: Alger Hiss on TV Panel
      Discussion." Time 80 (November 23, 1962): 69.

340. "Untold Story of Nixon on the Press." U.S. News and
      World Report 53 (November 26, 1962): 46+.

1964 Presidential Campaign

341. "Compromise Candidate?" U.S. News and World Report 55
      (August 12, 1963): 10.

342. Donovan, Robert J. "Over-nominated, Under-elected,
      Still a Promising Candidate." New York Times
      Magazine (April 25, 1965): 14-15+.

343. Evans, Rowland, and Robert D. Novak. "Unmaking of a
      President." Esquire 62 (November 1964); 90-92+.

344. Moley, Raymond. "Nixon's Role in 1964." Newsweek 64
      (October 26, 1964): 124.

345. "Non-candidate Nixon." Newsweek 63 (February 24,
      1964): 20-21.

346. "Return to the Wars." Time 84 (October 9, 1964): 25-
      26.

347. "Richard Nixon's Return." Commonweal 79 (October 18,
      1963): 87.

348. Weisbord, Marvin. Campaigning for President.
     Washington, DC: Public Affairs Press, 1964.

349. White, Theodore. The Making of the President, 1964.
     New York, NY: Atheneum, 1965.

350. "Will It Be Nixon vs Kennedy Again in '64?" U.S. News
     and World Report 35 (November 25, 1963); 34-35.

1966 Congressional Campaign

351. "Nixon and the GOP: Comeback?" Newsweek 68 (October
     10, 1966): 30-35.

352. "Nixon on the Move: Is His Eye on '68 Campaign?"
     U.S. News and World Report 59 (September 24,
     1965): 19.

353. Witcover, Jules. "Availability of Richard Nixon."
     Reporter 35 (August 11, 1966): 27-29.

1968 Presidential Campaign

354. Alexander, Herbert E. Financing the 1968 Election.
     Jackson, MS: University of Mississippi Press,
     1971.

355. Balfour, Nancy. "Nixon's the One for America." World
     Today 24 (November 1968): 467-475.

356. Burnham, Walter D. "Election 1968--The Abortive
     Landslide." Transaction 6, 2 (1968): 18-24.

357. Chester, Lewis, et al. An American Melodrama: The
     Presidential Campaign of 1968. New York, NY:
     Viking Press, 1969.

358. Converse, Philip E., et al. "Continuity and Change in
     American Politics: Parties and Issues in the 1968
     Election." American Political Science Review 63
     (December 1968); 1083-1115.

359. Coveyou, Michael R., and David G. Pfeiffer.
     "Education and Voting Turnout of Blacks in the
     1968 Presidential Election." Journal of Politics
     35 (November 1973): 795-1001.

360. Craig, George M. "The Campaign, Nixon and the American Atlantic Policy." International Journal 24 (Spring 1969): 302-309.

361. Duncan, David Douglas. "Inside the Nixon Campaign: Photographs." Newsweek 72 (August 19, 1968): 33-37.

362. English, David. Divided They Stand. Englewood Cliffs, NJ: Prentice-Hall, 1969.

363. Frost, David. The Presidential Debates, 1968. New York, NY: Stein and Day, 1968.

364. Goodman, Walter. "1968". Commentary 48 (December 1968): 83-86.

365. Graber, Doris A. "Press Coverage and Voter Reaction in the 1968 Presidential Election." Political Science Quarterly 89 (March 1974): 68-100.

366. Harrison, Gilbert A. "Richard Nixon's Return Engagement." New Republic 157 (November 4, 1967); 11-12.

367. Hess, Stephen, and David S. Broder. The Republican Establishment: the Present and the Future of the GOP. New York, NY: Harper and Row, 1967.

368. _____. "What Keeps Nixon Running?" Harpers 235 (August 1967); 56-58+.

369. Howe, Russell W., and Sarah H. Trott. "The Truth at Last: How Nixon Beat Humphrey." Washington Monthly 8 (December 1976): 50-53.

370. "Incredible '68: Year of Comeback." Life 66 (January 10, 1969): 58-59.

371. Just, Ward S. "Campaigning: Nixon." Atlantic 222 (July 1968): 44.

372. Kilpatrick, James J. "Crisis Seven." National Review 19 (November 14, 1967): 1263-1274.

373. _____. "Random Notes from the Campaign Trail." National Review 20 (December 3, 1968): 1210-1212+.

374. Kirkpatrick, Samuel A., and Melvin E. Jones. "Vote Direction and Issue Cleavage in 1968." _Social Science Quarterly_ 51 (December 1970): 689-705.

375. Knappman, Edward W. _Presidential Election 1968_. New York, NY: Facts on File, 1970.

376. McGinniss, Joe. _Selling of the President 1968_. New York, NY: Trident Press, 1969.

377. Mailer, Norman. _Miami and the Siege of Chicago_. New York, NY: Signet Books, 1968.

378. Meyer, Frank S. "Mandate of 1968." _National Review_ 20 (November 19, 1968): 1170.

379. Morin, Relman. _The Associated Press Story of Election 1968_. New York, NY: Pocket Books, 1969.

380. Mustafa, Zubeida. "The American Presidential Election, 1968." _Pakistan Horizon_ 22 (Fall 1969): 54-57.

381. "New Image for Nixon?" _American_ 118 (February 3, 1968): 138.

382. "Nixon Looks to November: Here Is His Strategy." _U.S. News and World Report_ 65 (July 29, 1968): 28-29.

383. "Nixon Story: Political Comeback of the Century." _U.S. News and World Report_ 65 (November 18, 1968): 92-95.

384. Polsby, Nelson W. _The Citizen's Choice: Humphrey or Nixon_. Washington, DC: Public Affairs Press, 1968.

385. "The Public Record of Richard M. Nixon." _Congressional Quarterly Weekly Report_ 25 (June 23, 1967): 1081-1091.

386. Reichley, James. "How Nixon Plans to Bring It Off." _Fortune_ 76 (December 1967): 124-127+.

387. Reiss, Albert. "Commment: Crime, Law and Order as Election Issues." _Transaction_ 5, 10 (1968): 2-4.

388. "Richard Nixon, Will He Win?" _U.S. News and World Report_ 65 (August 19, 1968): 23-32.

389. Robers, Myran. The Begatting of a President. New
      York, NY: Ballantine Books, 1969.

390. Schapp, Dick. "Will Richard Nixon Trip over Himself
      on His Way to Victory?" New York (June 10, 1968):
      24.

391. Schreiber, E.M. "Vietnam Policy Preferences and
      Withheld 1968 Presidential Votes." Public Opinion
      Quarterly 37 (Spring 1973): 91-98.

392. "Secret of the Nixon Comeback: Years of Hard Work."
      U.S. News and World Report 65 (August 19, 1968):
      30-31.

393. Shadegg, Stephen C. Winning's a Lot More Fun.
      London, UK: Macmillan, 1969.

394. Shannon, William V. "Richard Nixon Returns."
      Commonweal 87 (March 8, 1968): 677-678.

395. Steinem, Gloria. "In Your Heart You Know He's Nixon."
      New York (October 28, 1968): 20.

396. Wainwright, Loudon. "One More Try for the Heights."
      Life 64 (March 1, 1968): 6-62+.

397. "War, Welfare, and Richard Nixon." Nations Business
      55 (November 1967): 61-62+.

398. Whalen, Richard J. Catch the Falling Flag. Boston,
      MA: Houghton Mifflin Co., 1972.

399. White, Theodore. Making of the President, 1968. New
      York, NY: Atheneum, 1969.

400. Wildavsky, Aaron. "Richard Nixon: President of the
      United States." Transaction 5, 10 (1968): 8-15.

401. "Will It Be Nixon vs LBJ in '68?" U.S. News and World
      Report 61 (October 3, 1966): 54-58.

402. Wills, George. "What Makes the Newest Nixon Run? The
      Old Nixon?" Esquire 69 (May 1968): 89-96+.

403. Witcover, Jules. "Nixon: the Reentry Program." New
      Republic 156 (June 17, 1967): 11-12.

404. _____. "Nixon for President in '68?" Saturday
      Evening Post 240 (February 25, 1967): 93-97.

405. Wright, Gerald C. "Black Voting Turnout and Education
      in the 1968 Presidential Election." _Journal of
      Politics_ 37 (May 1975): 563-568.

1970 Congressional Campaign

406. Lees, John D. "Campaigns and Parties--the 1970
      American Midterm Elections and Beyond."
      Parliamentary Affairs 24 (Autumn 1971): 312-320.

407. Reichley, James. "That Elusive Political Majority."
      Fortune 83 (March 1971): 68-73+.

408. Rilling, Paul M. "Have Time and Reality Overtaken the
      Southern Strategy?" _Interplay_ 3 (August 1970):
      34-38.

409. "Selling the President, 1970." _Newsweek_ 76 (November
      16, 1970): 77-78.

410. "70 Campaign Takes a New Turn." _U.S. News and World
      Report_ 69 (October 26, 1970): 15-16.

411. Tindall, George B. "Southern Strategy: A Historical
      Perspective." _North Carolina Historical Review_ 48
      (April 1971): 126-141.

1972 Presidential Campaign

412. "After the Landslide: Nixon's Mandate." _Time_ 100
      (November 20, 1972): 14-16.

413. Alexander, Herbert E. _Financing the 1972 Election_.
      Lexington, MA: Lexington Books, 1976.

414. Alsop, Stewart. "Nixon and the Square Majority."
      Atlantic 229 (February 1972): 41-47.

415. Auspitz, Josiah Lee. "Why Nixon Needs Brooke." _Ripon
      Forum_ 8 (January 1972): 8-14.

416. Bell, B. Tartt. "The Campaign for the White House--
      1972." _Contemporary Review_ 221 (October 1972):
      177-183.

417. Bonafede, Dom. "Nixon Models Campaign Organization
      After His Successful Version of 1968." _National_

Journal (September 11, 1971): 1876-1884.

418. _____. "Nixon Strategy Calls for Low-Key Campaign with Strong Emphasis on Performance." _National Journal_ 4 (April 22, 1972): 672-679.

419. Brown, Clifford W. _Jaw of Victory: the Game Plan Politics of 1972, the Crisis of the Republican Party and the Future of the Constitution._ Boston, MA: Brown, Little and Company, 1974.

420. "Campaign 72: Newspaper Endorsements: Nixon, 753; McGovern, 56." _Congressional Quarterly-Weekly Report_ 30 (November 1972): 2898-2899.

421. "The Candidate and the Cities." _Nation's Cities_ 10 (October 1972): 12-13+.

422. Clarke, John H., et al. "Editorial: The Presidential Election, A Victory for Racism." _Freedomways_ 12 (Fall 1972): 269-272.

423. Dela Isla, Jose. "The Politics of Reflection: Se Habla Espanol." _Aztlan_ 7, 3 (1979): 427-451.

424. Donahue, Bernard F. "The Political Use of Religious Symbols: A Case Study of the 1972 Presidential Campaign." _Review of Politics_ 37 (January 1975): 48-65.

425. Evarts, Dru, and Guido Stempel. "Coverage of the 1972 Campaign by TV, News Magazines, and Major Newspapers." _Journalism Quarterly_ 51 (Winter 1974): 645-648.

426. Fisher, Walter R. "Reaffirmation and Subversion of the American Dream." _Quarterly Journal of Speech_ 59 (April 1973): 160-167.

427. Gillette, Robert. "Scientists in Politics: A Late Entry for Nixon's Group." _Science_ 178 (October 1972): 375-377.

428. Graber, Doris A. "Effect of Incumbency on Coverage Patterns in 1972 Presidential Campaign." _Journalism Quarterly_ 53 (Autumn 1976): 499-508.

429. _____. "Personal Qualities in Presidential Images: The Contributions of the Press." _Midwest Journal of Political Science_ 16 (February 1972): 46-76.

430. Greene, Bob. Running: A Nixon-McGovern Campaign
          Journal. Chicago, IL: Henry Regnery Company,
          1973.

431. Harrington, Michael. "Negative Landslide: The Myth
          That Was Real." Nation 215 (November 27, 1972):
          418-521.

432. Hofstetter, C. Richard, and Cliff Zukin. "Network
          News and Advertising in the Nixon and McGovern
          Campaigns." Journalism Quarterly 56 (Spring
          1979): 106-115, 152.

433. Jacobson, Gary C. "Presidential Coattails in 1972."
          Public Opinion Quarterly 40 (Summer 1976): 194-
          200.

434. James, Judson L., and Dorothy B. James. "Lessons of
          Watergate: The Nixon Campaigns." Current
          History 67 (July 1974): 31-33; 38.

435. Levine, Arthur. "I Got My Job Through CREEP."
          Washington Monthly 6 (November 1974): 35-46.

436. Lurie, Leonard. The Running of Richard Nixon. New
          York NY: Coward, McCann and Geoghegan, 1972.

437. McKenzie, Richard B., and Bruce Yandle. "The Logic of
          Irrational Politics: Nixon's Reelection
          Committee." Public Finance Quarterly 8 (January
          1980): 39-55.

438. Martinson, David L. "Coverage of La Follette Offers
          Insights for 1972 Campaign." Journalism Quarterly
          52 (Autumn 1975): 539-542.

439. Meadow, Robert G. "Cross Comparison of Coverage of
          the 1972 Presidential Campaign." Journalism
          Quarterly 50 (Autumn 1973): 482-488.

440. Miller, Arthur H., Warren E. Miller, Alden S. Raine,
          and Thad A. Brown. "A Majority Party in Disarray:
          Policy Polarization in the 1972 Election."
          American Political Science Review 70 (September
          1976): 753-778.

441. Murphey, Reg. The Southern Strategy. New York, NY:
          Charles Scribner's, 1971.

442. Myers, David S. "Editorials and Foreign Affairs in
      the 1972 Presidential Campaign." Journal
      Quarterly 51 (Summer 1974): 251-257.

443. Nicholas, H.G. "The 1972 Elections." Journal of
      American Studies 7 (April 1973): 1-15.

444. "Nixon and McGovern on the Issues." U.S. News and
      World Report 73 (November 6, 1972): 28-31.

445. "Nixon Campaign: Mounting a Drive for Another Term."
      Congressional Quarterly-Weekly Report 29 (November
      27, 1971): 2452-2457.

446. "Nixon's Chances in '72 as The Republicans See Them."
      U.S. News and World Report 71 (August 9, 1971):
      37-39.

447. "Nixon's Strategy for '72." U.S. News and World
      Report 69 (November 28, 1970): 21-24.

448. Nolan, Martin F. "Reselling to the President: PR men
      in the White House." Atlanta 230 (November 1972):
      79-81.

449. "Old Nixon or the New Nixon for 1972?" Economist 241
      (December 4, 1971): 55-56.

450. Pearl, Arthur. Landslide: the How and Why of Nixon's
      Victory. Secaucus, NJ: Citadel Press, 1973.

451. Pei, Mario. "The Language of the Election and
      Watergate Years." Modern Age 17 (Fall 1973):
      387-398.

452. Perry, James M. Us and Them: How the Press Covered
      the 1972 Election. New York, NY: Clarkson N.
      Potter, 1973.

453. Podhoretz, Norman. "Between Nixon and the New
      Politics." Commentary 54 (September 1972): 4-8.

454. Pomper, Gerald M. "Nixon and the End of Presidential
      Politics." Society 10 (March/April 1973): 14-16.

455. Real, Michael R. "Popular Culture, Media Propaganda,
      and the 1972 CREEP Campaign." Journal of Popular
      Culture 8 (Winter 1974): 644-652.

456. Reeves, Richard. "How Nixon Outwits the Press." New
      York Magazine 5 (October 9, 1972): 49-52+.

457. Riegle, Donald Wayne. "Dump Nixon Campaign." Look 35
      (June 1, 1971): 79-80.

458. Roback, Thomas H. "Amateurs and Professional:
      Delegates to the 1972 Republican National
      Convention." Journal of Political 37 (May 1975):
      436-468.

459. Sidney, Hugh. "The Big Win: What Will Nixon Do with
      It?" Life 73 (November 1972): 4-8.

460. Soderlund, Walter C., and Ronald H. Wagenberg. "A
      Context Analysis of Editorial Coverage of the 1972
      Election Campaigns in Canada and the United
      States." Western Political Quarterly 28 (March
      1975): 85-107.

461. Truscott, L.K. "Coronation of Richard Nixon."
      Saturday Review 55 (September 16, 1972): 7-8+.

462. Weichkardt, George G. "Income Maintenance: Nixon's
      FAP McGovern's UTC, the New British Proposal and a
      Recommendation." Harvard Journal of Legislation
      10 (June 1973): 672-714.

463. White, Theodore. The Making of a President, 1972.
      New York, NY: Atheneum, 1973.

464. Wilson, Graham K., and Philip M. Williams. "Mr.
      Nixon's Triumph." Parliamentary Affairs 26
      (Spring 1973); 186-200.

465. Wimberly, Ronald L. "Civil Religion and the Choice
      for President: Nixon in '72." Social Forces 59
      (September 1980): 44-61.

466. Zoll, Donald A. "A Prospectus for a Conservative
      Majority." Modern Age 17, 4 (1973); 368-377.

1974 Congressional Campaign

467. Adamany, David, and George Agree. "Election Campaign
      Financing: The 1974 Reforms." Political Science
      Quarterly 90 (Summer 1975): 201-220.

468. McLeod, Jack M., et al. "Watergate and the 1974
      Reforms." Political Science Quarterly 90 (Summer
      1975): 201-220.

469.   Pierson, J.   "Presidential Popularity and Midterm
          Voting at Different Electoral Levels."   Journal of
          Political Studies 19 (November 1975): 683-694.

470.   Uslaner, Eric M., and M. Margaret Conway.   "The
          Responsible Congressional Electorate: Watergate,
          the Economy, and Vote Choice in 1974."   American
          Political Science Review 79 (September 1985):
          788-803.

Campaign Speeches

471.   "Academic Freedom (Address on June 5, 1966)."   Vital
          Speeches 32 (July 1, 1966):   550-552.

472.   "Acceptance Speech at Republican National Convention
          on August 8, 1968."   Vital Speeches 34 (September
          1, 1968):   674-677.

473.   "Acceptance Speech at Republican National Convention
          on August 23, 1972."   Vital Speeches 38 (September
          15, 1972):   706-709.

474.   "Ahead with Ike or back to '52 (Address on October 19,
          1954)."   U.S. News and World Report 37 (October
          29, 1954):   99-100+.

475.   "American Policy Abroad (address on April 20, 1963)."
          Vital Speeches 29 (June 1, 1963):   486-490.

476.   "Elections Spotlights Nixon Position on Libraries
          (statement on October 22, 1968)."   Library Journal
          93 (December 1, 1968):   44-61.

477.   "Equality Under the Law (address on October 18,
          1956)."   Vital Speeches 22 (November 1, 1956):
          38-40.

478.   "Firm Line on Reds, Strong Defense, No Appeasement
          (address on September 6, 1956)."   U.S. News and
          World Report 65 (September 16, 1968): 48.

479.   "From Informal Talks, Nixon's View of the World
          (remarks on August 9, 1968)."   U.S. News and World
          Report 65 (September 16, 1968):   48.

480. "Goals of a New Administration (address on July 28,
        1960)." U.S. News and World Report 49 (August 8,
        1966): 194-197.

481. "Hard Lines and Guidelines (address on December 3,
        1956)." Vital Speeches 32 (January 15, 1966):
        194-197.

482. "How Nixon Sees the Presidency (address on September
        1968)." Newsweek 72 (September 30, 1968): 24-25.

483. "Meaning of the Hiss Case." Readers' Digest 61
        (November 1952): 55-60.

484. "My Side of the Story." Vital Speeches 19 (October
        15, 1952): 11-15.

485. "Nature of the Presidency (address on September 19,
        1968)." Vital Speeches 35 (October 15, 1968): 6-
        8.

486. "New Beginning (address on February 3, 1968)." Vital
        Speeches 34 (March 1, 1968): 299-300.

487. "Nixon Calls for War on Crime Before It Is Too Late
        (statement on May 9, 1968)." U.S. News and World
        Report 64 (May 20, 1968): 98.

488. "Nixon on Racial Accommodation (excerpts from
        address)." Time 91 (May 3, 1968): 21.

489. "Nixon on the Cities' Crisis (excerpt from radio
        address on May 2, 1968)." U.S. News and World
        Report 64 (May 13, 1968): 21.

490. "Nixon on the Presidency (excerpts from address in
        September 1968)." Time 92 (September 27, 1968):
        18.

491. "Nixon Speaks About Scientists." Science 162
        (December 13, 1968): 1253.

492. "Nixon Spells out the Republican Goals (address on
        August 23, 1956)." Vital Speeches 22 (September
        15, 1956): 706-708.

493. "Nixon's First Statement, September 18, 1952." U.S.
        News and World Report 33 (October 3, 1952): 61.

72

494. "Our Partnership in Creating a World of Peace,
     (address on July 16, 1956)." Vital Speeches 22
     (August 1, 1956): 610-612.

495. "Plea for an Anti-communist Faith." Saturday Review
     35 (May 24, 1952): 12.

496. "Promise of the American Revolution (address on
     September 6, 1958)." Vital Speeches 24 (September
     15, 1958): 717-720.

497. "We Have a Job to Do, (address July 11, 1952)." Vital
     Speeches 18 (August 1, 1952): 611-612.

498. "What the Candidates Would Do About Black Capitalism
     (excerpts from address on April 25, 1968)." U.S.
     News and World Report 65 (September 30, 1968):
     65.

499. Wills, Garry. "The Checkers Speech (reprint)."
     Esquire 99 (June 1983): 122-124+.

Vice-Presidency

Richard Nixon was a successful vice-president. On
three occasions, Nixon had to perform the responsibilities
of the president while Dwight Eisenhower recovered his
health. Each of these occasions was without benefit of the
Twenty-Fifth Amendment to the Constitution, which now
prescribes the procedures for the vice-president to assume
the president's duties if the president is incapacitated by
ill health. Nixon carefully performed the president's
responsibilities without conveying an impression of "taking
over" and without serious consequences to the nation's
domestic and foreign affairs. In 1955, Nixon was lauded by
Robert Rovere in an article for the New Yorker entitled
"Letter from Washington: National Security Council and
Cabinet Under Direction from Mr. Nixon," for his calm,
objective handling of a politically sensitive action. In
1957, when Nixon was again called upon to handle
presidential duties for an ill Eisenhower, political
analysts found his actions praiseworthy. The comment "New
Nixon Gains Sature in His Latest Test," reported by Business
Week, was typical.

Within a year of the 1952 presidential campaign,
Newsweek made the comment that "Richard Nixon has made

something of the vice-presidency." This sentiment was
restated in 1968 by Michael Dorman in his work, The Second
Man: the Changing Role of the Vice Presidency. In his
work, Dorman details Nixon's role as vice-president:
handling the three health crises of Eisenhower's presidency,
chairing important executive branch committees, visiting 54
foreign nations, acting as the liaison between the president
and congress, and serving as the Republican Party chief
political campaigner. Nixon's role as an active, involved
vice-president has become the mode for many subsequent vice-
presidents, and thus the modern role model for the office.

During the years in which Richard Nixon was vice-
president several important events occurred which became key
elements in making Nixon the leading candidate to succeed
Eisenhower as president. In 1958, Nixon made a state visit
to several Latin American countries. While in Venezuela,
Nixon, as the symbol of American policies toward Latin
America, was attacked by a mob of angry demonstrators.
Nixon's courage in standing up to the demonstrators and
defending American policy is detailed in news reports of the
period such as "Hail the Hero," which appeared in a May 1958
issue of the Nation. "I Saw Nixon Mobbed," U.S. News and
World Report, appeared in May of 1958. Nixon's role in the
Latin American demonstrations was viewed as that of defender
of the nation's policies in foreign lands. Equally
beneficial to Nixon's political career was the famous

"Kitchen debate" between Nixon and Nikita Krushchev, the
Soviet Premier, at a U.S. exhibition in Moscow. Again,
Nixon appeared to be the defender of American principles and
policies in a foreign land. He received praise for his
action as evinced in "Nixon and Krushchev Go into Action,"
which appeared in U.S. News and World Report in August of
1959.

However, the role Nixon eagerly accepted as political
pitchman for the Republican Party during the Eisenhower
presidency earned him great criticism. The New Republic
described Nixon as "hero and heavy" in November of 1958.
Harpers wondered in print "Nixon: What Kind of President?"
in a 1959 issue. Time gave the analysis "Old Nixon, New
Magic," in October of 1958. Paul C. Light in his Vice-
Presidential Power (1984) provided the historical assessment
for Nixon's political role as vice-president. Light argued
tht Nixon first saw the potential of the political role of
the vice-presidency and so shaped that role for the second
half of the twentieth century.

500. "Acting Captain." Time 66 (October 10, 1955): 23-26.

501. Adkinson, Danny M. "The Vice Presidency as
     Apprenticeship." Presidential Studies Quarterly
     13 (Spring 1983): 212-218.

502. "Africans Are Pleased to Meet Nixon." Life 42 (March
     25, 1957): 40-41.

503. "Again the New Nixon." Nation 188 (May 2, 1959): 398.

504. "As Nixon Tours Latin America." US News and World
     Report 44 (May 9, 1958): 44.

505. "Broken Glass and Tacks on Nixon's Path." New
     Republic 133 (October 17, 1955): 3-5.

506. "Bulwark Against Communism." Commonweal 61 (March 4,
     1955): 572-573.

507. Buryan, Patrick. "Vice-President Nixon."
     Contemporary Review 190 (July 1956): 14-17.

508. Cater, Douglass. "Nixon for Nixon." Reporter 19
     (November 13, 1958): 20-21.

509. _____. "Who Is Nixon, What Is He?" Reporter 19
     (November 27, 1958): 9-13.

510. "Changing Africa." America 97 (April 20, 1957): 62-
     63.

511. Collins, Frederick William. "Presenting the 1960
     Nixon." Nation 185 (November 23, 1957): 381-382.

512. Coughlan, Robert. "Debate, Pro and Con, Subject:
     Richard M. Nixon." Life 41 (July 16, 1956): 92-
     93+.

513. _____. "Success Story of a Vice-president." Life
     35 (December 14, 1953): 146-148+.

514. "Crucial Position of Nixon." Life 43 (September 30,
     1957): 26-27.

515. "Debating Foreign Policy." Commonweal 69 (October 31,
     1958): 117-118.

516. DeToledano, Ralph. "Different Nixon of '56."
     Newsweek 48 (October 1, 1956): 25-27.

517. Dorman, Michael. The Second Man: the Changing Role
     of the Vice-Presidency. New York, NY: Delacorte
     Press, 1968. pp. 198-241.

518. Erskine, Helen W. "Dick and Pat Nixon: The Team on
     Ike's Team." Colliers (July 9, 1954): 32-37.

519. "Eye of the Hurricane: Nixon Saga: Cartoonists'
     View." Time 67 (March 26, 1956): 21-23.

520. "For South America: Nixon's Smile and US Help?" US
      News and World Report 44 (May 2, 1958): 35.

521. Galloway, Charles H. "I Saw Nixon Mobbed." US News
      and World Report 44 (May 23, 1958): 48-49.

522. "Guests of Venezuela." Time 71 (May 26, 1958): 36-37.

523. "Hail the Hero." Nation 186 (May 24, 1958): 36-37.

524. Halsey, Margaret. "Beware the Tender Trap." New
      Republic 138 (January 13, 1958): 7-9.

525. Harrison, Selig S. "Nixon: The Old Guard's Young
      Pretender." New Republic 135 (August 20, 1956):
      9-15.

526. "Hate Running Loose Hits Out at Nixon." Life 44 (May
      26, 1958): 32-38.

527. Healy, Diana D. America's Vice-Presidents. New York,
      NY: Atheneum, 1984. pp. 192-197.

528. Healy, Paul F. "Busiest Vice-President We Ever Had."
      Saturday Evening Post 226 (September 19, 1983):
      22-23.

529. Houston, Ernest. "What's Wrong with Nixon?" New
      Republic 138 (June 16, 1958): 23.

530. "How Europe Sized up the Nixon Trip." US News and
      World Report 47 (August 10, 1959): 72-73.

531. "How Nixon Tells US story Abroad." US News and World
      Report 44 (May 16, 1958): 47-48.

532. Howe, Irving. "Poor Richard Nixon." New Republic 134
      (May 7, 1956): 7-9.

533. "Ike's Man Friday." Newsweek 52 (December 22, 1957):
      16.

534. "In a Position to Help." Time 70 (December 9, 1957):
      23-26.

535. "Inside Story of Fight Against Nixon; Battle Stassen
      Started, Blow-by-Blow Account." US News and World
      Report 41 (August 3, 1956): 34-38+.

536. Knebel, Fletcher. "Did Ike Really Want Nixon?" Look
      20 (October 30, 1956): 25-27.

537. Light, Paul C. "The Institutional Vice Presidency."
     Presidential Studies Quarterly 13 (Spring 1983):
     198-211.

538. _____. Vice Presidential Power. Baltimore, MD:
     Johns Hopkins University Press, 1984.

539. Los Angeles Times--The Nixons in South America. Los
     Angeles, CA: Los Angeles Times, 1958.

540. Maung, Maung. "Richard Nixon in Rangoon." New
     Republic 129 (December 14, 1953): 22.

541. "Mr. Nixon and Our Good Neighbors." America 99 (May
     24, 1958): 251.

542. "Mr. Nixon's Visit to Krushchev." London News 235
     (August 5, 1959): 20-21.

543. Moley, Robert. "Lilliputian Regency." Newsweek 50
     (December 16, 1957): 124.

544. Morgan, Edward P. "Reported with Nixon: Visit to
     Russia." New Republic 141 (August 24, 1959): 7-
     8.

545. "New Nixon Gains Stature in His Latest Test."
     Business Week (December 7, 1957): 28-29.

546. "Nixon: Political Sinecure Becomes a Success Story."
     Newsweek 42 (October 5, 1953): 29+.

547. "Nixon: A Working Job as Vice-President?" US News
     and World Report 35 (November 14, 1952): 55-56.

548. "Nixon Africanus." Time 69 (March 11, 1957): 16.

549. "Nixon and a Cure?" Newsweek 51 (May 26, 1958): 24-
     26.

550. "Nixon and His Critics." Commonweal 70 (August 14,
     1959): 411-412.

551. "Nixon and Krushchev Go into Action." US News and
     World Report 47 (August 10, 1959): 82-83.

552. "Nixon and the People." Commonweal 69 (October 10,

553. "Nixon and The Recession." Newsweek 51 (March 24,
      1958): 32.

554. "Nixon's Own Ordeal in Latin America: May 1958." US
      News and World Report 66 (June 16, 1969): 32.

555. "Nixon: At Home and Abroad." Commonweal 69 (December
      12, 1958): 280.

556. "Nixon Begins His Grueling Duties." Life 43 (December
      9, 1957): 38-39.

557. "Nixon: Front and Center." New Republic 139 (October
      13, 1958): 2.

558. "Nixon: Hero and Heavy." New Republic 139 (November
      3, 1958): 3.

559. "Nixon Issue." Harper 211 (September 1955): 20-22.

560. "Nixon on Africa." US News and World Report 42 (April
      12, 1957): 18.

561. "Nixon, Once Soviet Guest, Becomes Top Soviet Target."
      US News and World Report 47 (September 28, 1959):
      58-60.

562. "Nixon Shakes Hands, Wins Asians." US News and World
      Report 35 (December 4, 1953): 37-40.

563. "Nixon Story." US News and World Report 40 (May 11,
      1956): 68-72+.

564. "Nixon: The Real No. 2 Man." US News and World
      Report 35 (October 2, 1953): 43-45.

565. "Nixon's New Role." US News and World Report 43
      (December 6, 1957): 48-53.

566. "Nixon's Own Story of Seven Years in the Vice-
      Presidency." US News and World Report 48 (May 16,
      1960): 98-106.

567. "Nixon's Own Story of His Trip." US News and World
      Report 44 (May 30, 1958): 8.

568. "Old Nixon, New Magic." Time 72 (October 13, 1958):
      19-20.

569.   "Political Dramatics."   Commonweal 68 (May 16, 1958):
       172-173.

570.   "Political Schizophrenia."   Commonweal 67 (February 7,
       1958):   476-477.

571.   "Power Struggle on the Road to the White House."   US
       News and World Report 44 (March 28, 1958):   70-72.

572.   Riggs, Robert L.   "No Troubles in Our House: Nixon's
       Kentucky Campaign."   New Republic 131 (October 25,
       1954):   8-9.

573.   Rivera-Torres, Miguel.   "Latin American Exile on
       Nixon's Tour."   Reporter 17 (November 14, 1957):
       23-25.

574.   Rovere, Robert H.   "Letter from Washington: National
       Security Council and Cabinet Under Direction of
       Mr. Nixon."   The New Yorker 31 (October 8, 1955):
       179-186+.

575.   _____.   "Nixon: Most Likely to Succeed."   Harper
       211 (September 1955):   57-63.

576.   Rubottom, Robert R.   "Vice-President's Visit to South
       America in Perspective."   US Department of State
       Bulletin 38 (June 30, 1958):   1104-1109.

577.   Safford, Jeffrey J.   "The Nixon-Castro Meeting of 19
       April 1959."   Diplomatic History 4 (Winter 1980):
       425-431.

578.   Savage, Charles H.   "American Reports on on the
       Caracas Incident."   America 99 (May 31, 1958):
       290.

579.   Sherman, George.   "Afterthoughts on Nixon and
       Exhibition."   New Republic 141 (September 21,
       1959):   6-7.

580.   "Vice President Goes Abroad."   Time 62 (December 7,
       1953):   32-33.

581.   "Vice-President in Russia: A Brainstorming
       Masterpiece."   Life 47 (August 10, 1959):   22-25.

582.   "What Mikoyan Said to Nixon and Nixon to Mikoyan."   US
       News and World Report 46 (January 23, 1959): 88-
       89.

583. "What Nixon Learned in Russia." US News and World
      Report 47 (August 10, 1959): 37-39.

584. "When Nixon Took on Krushchev." US News and World
      Report 47 (August 3, 1959): 36-37.

585. White, William Smith. "Nixon: What Kind of
      President." Harper 216 (January 1958): 25-30.

586. Wilson, Richard L. "Big Changes in Richard Nixon."
      Look 21 (September 3, 1957): 66-69.

587. _____. "Is Nixon Fit to Be President?" Look 17
      (February 24, 1953): 33-42.

588. "With Nixon in Africa: Close-up of a New Nation." US
      News and World Report 42 (March 15, 1957): 78-81.

Speeches

589. "Appraisal of Summit Conference (address on April 23,
      1960)." Vital Speeches 26 (June 1, 1960): 484-
      486.

590. "Blunt Challenge to Our Free World (address on
      November 24, 1957)." Vital Speeches 24 (December
      15, 1957): 130-131.

591. "Boom to Continue for Business and Labor (address
      October 19, 1955)." US News and World Report 39
      (October 28, 1955): 85-89.

592. "Challenge to American Education (address on December
      15, 1957)." School and Society 86 (March 1,
      1958): 103-104.

593. "Chances for Peace Today (address October 17, 1955)."
      Vital Speeches 22 (November 15, 1955): 70-73.

594. "Differences That Divide Us (address on June 29,
      1959)." Vital Speeches 25 (August 15, 1959):
      644-645.

595. "Events in the Middle East (address on July 19,
      1958)." Vital Speeches 24 (August 1, 1958): 615-
      619.

596. "Government Policy in Present Recession (address on
     April 24, 1958)." Vital Speeches 24 (May 15,
     1958): 464-467.

597. "Latin America today." Vital Speeches 21 (April 15,
     1955): 1154-1159.

598. "Mr. Nixon Attacks Communist Conspirators (excerpts
     from address on August 31, 1953)." US News and
     World Report 35 (September 11, 1953): 28+.

599. "New Approach by the US in Fighting Communism (excerpt
     from address on August 2, 1954)." US News and
     World Report (August 13, 1954): 26-27.

600. "New Soviet Tactics." Vital Speeches 22 (July 1,
     1956): 546-549.

601. "Nikita S. Khrushchev: The Man and His Mission
     (address on September 14, 1959)." Vital Speeches
     26 (October 15, 1959): 15-18.

602. "Policies of the American Government and People
     (address on August 1, 1959)." Vital Speeches 25
     (September 1, 1959): 679-682.

603. "Private Investment and the Economic Challenge
     (address on October 15, 1957)." US Department of
     State Bulletin 37 (November 4, 1957): 703-707.

604. "Responsibility of the English-speaking Peoples in
     Preserving Peace and Freedom (address on November
     26, 1958)." US Department of State Bulletin 40
     (January 5, 1959): 14-17.

605. "Rule of Law for Nations (address on April 13, 1959)."
     Vital Speeches 25 (May 1, 1959): 421-424.

606. "Setting Russia Straight on Facts about the US
     (address on July 24, 1959)." US News and World
     Report 47 (August 3, 1959): 7072.

607. "United States--Brazilian Friendship (address on
     February 3, 1956)." US Department of State
     Bulletin 34 (February 27, 1956): 335-338.

608. "United States--Latin American Relations (address on
     May 21, 1958)." Vital Speeches 24 (June 15,
     1958): 514-519.

609. "Vice President Nixon Opens American Exhibition at
      Moscow (arrival address on July 23, 1959)." US
      Department of State Bulletin 41 (August 17,
      1959).

610. "Vice President Outlines US Policy Abroad (address on
      December 6, 1956)." Vital Speeches 23 (January 1,
      1957): 162-165.

Presidency (General)

There can be no doubt that Richard Milhous Nixon's presidency failed. The Watergate scandal, impeachment hearings, and Nixon's resignation condemn the Nixon presidency to an image of failure. But, there are, within the four years preceding the Watergate scandal, several important domestic and foreign initatives that bring the Nixon presidency an image of strength and success to haunt and frustrate the researcher. With Nixon (1977) by Raymond Price emphasizes that, in addition to the Watergate scandal, there was great substance in Nixon's welfare reform, executive branch reorganization, wage and price regulation, peace in Vietnam, and the China reassessment. Rowland Evans and Robert Novak also examine the accomplishments of the Nixon presidency in their work, Nixon in the White House: the Frustration of Power (1971).

A complete assessment of the Nixon presidency will not be likely to occur until the rhetoric and politics of the Watergate scandal are forgotten. But tentative assessments of the Nixon presidency have been made. In 1970, Newsweek published "Historians Rate Mr. Nixon," in which the Nixon presidency is examined by leading historians who focus upon domestic and foreign accomplishments. Peter Jenkins,

anticipating Nixon's impeachment in May of 1974, wrote
"Portrait of a Presidency," for the New Statesman in which
he labelled the entire Nixon presidency as "dishonest,
disgraceful, and inept." Following this thought, Henry
Abraham wrote, "The Presidency at the Threshold of the Last
Quarter Century" for the Southern Quarterly in 1977 in which
he viewed the Nixon presidency as a personal affair that
operated from the conviction that it had a right to nullify
the constitution and law in order to achieve its policies.

An unlikely defender of the Nixon presidency
interjected a note of caution into the preliminary
assessments made soon after the presidential resignation in
August of 1974. Gore Vidal, a published critic of Richard
Nixon, wrote an assessment of the Nixon presidency in Fifty
Who Made the Difference (1984). Vidal speculated that
Richard Nixon could be viewed in the distant future as the
only great president of the last half of twentieth century
America. Vidal based his assessment upon Nixon's foreign
policy, which stressed peaceful co-existence with the Soviet
Union, exploitation of the differences between the Russian
and Chinese communist states, and a firm belief that the
United States was only one among many nations and not the
first among nations. This view of the Nixon presidency is
also stated in Robert Semple's "Richard M. Nixon: A
Tentative Evaluation," which appeared in Power and the
Presidency (1976). Respect for domestic actions taken by

the Nixon presidency is found in Richard Nathan's The
Administrative Presidency (1983).

611. Abraham, Henry J. "The Presidency at the Threshold of
      the Last Quarter Century." Southern Quarterly 15,
      3 (1977): 231-244.

612. Allen, Gary. Nixon's Palace Guard. Boston, MA:
      Western Island, 1971.

613. Alley, Robert S. So Help Me God: Religion and the
      Presidency, Wilson to Nixon. Richmond, VA: John
      Knox Press, 1972.

614. Alsop, Stewart. "Demonsterization of Nixon."
      Newsweek 73 (February 24, 1969): 104.

615. _____. "Nixon and the Square Majority." Atlantic
      229 (February 1972): 41-47.

616. Anderson, Jack, and George Clifford. The Anderson
      Papers. New York, NY: Random House, 1973.

617. Armbruster, Maxim E. "Richard Nixon." Presidents of
      the United States and Their Administrations from
      Washington To Nixon. New York, NY: Horizon
      Press, 1973. pp. 349-362.

618. Arnhart, Larry. "The God-like Prince: John Locke's
      Executive Prerogative and the American
      Presidency." Presidential Studies Quarterly 9, 2
      (Spring 1979): 121-130.

619. "At the Nixon Court: Presidential Intrigue." Nation
      217 (October 3, 1973): 324.

620. Atkins, Ollie. Triumph and Tragedy: The White House
      Years. New York, NY: Playboy Press, 1977.

621. Balfour, Nancy. "President Nixon at Mid-Term." World
      Today 26 (October 1970): 445-450.

622. _____. "President Nixon Sets the Stage." World
      Today 25 (March 1969): 96-102.

623. _____. "President Nixon with One Year to Go."
      World Today 27 (November 1971): 463-471.

624. _____. "President Nixon's Second Term. World Today 29 (March 1973): 98-107.

625. _____. "The US Presidency in Danger." World Today 29 (December 1973): 505-513.

626. Barber, James D. "American Redemption: The Presidential Character from Nixon to Ford to Carter." Washington Monthly 9 (April 1977): 8-18.

627. _____. "Analyzing Presidents: From Passive Positive Taft to Active-Negative Nixon." Washington Monthly 1 (October 1969): 33-54.

628. _____. "Man, Mood, and the Presidency." Rex G. Rugwell and Thomas E. Cronin, eds. The Presidency Reappraised. New York, NY: Praeger, 1974. pp. 205-214.

629. _____. "Nixon's brush with Tyranny." Political Science Quarterly 92 (Winter 1977-1978): 62-66.

630. _____. "Question of Presidential Character." Saturday Review 55 (September 23, 1972): 62-66.

631. _____. "Tone-deaf in the Oval Office." Saturday Review World 1 (January 12, 1974): 10-14.

632. Barthelmas, Wes, et al. "Four More Years." Commonweal 97 (December 1972): 198-209.

633. Barzman, Sol. "Richard Nixon." Madmen and Geniuses. New York, NY: Follett, 1974. pp. 253-260.

634. "Battle for the Mind of Nixon." Nation 208 (January 27, 1969): 98-99.

635. Beman, Lewis. "President Less Government in Washington." Fortune 89 (January 1974): 74-76+.

636. "Benchmarks to Judge Nixon by: Measuring the First Six Months." Life 67 (June 25, 1969): 30.

637. Berman, Bruce J. "Richard Nixon and the New Corporate State." Queen's Quarterly 80 (Autumn 1973): 425-433.

638. Bhagwati, Jagdish. "United States in the Nixon Era:
      The End of Innocence." Daedalus 101 (Fall 1972):
      25-47.

639. Brummet, Barry. "Presidential Substance: (the
      address of August 15, 1973)." Western Speech 39,
      (Fall 1975): 249-259.

640. Buchanan, Bruce. The Presidential Experience: What
      the Offce Does to the Man. Englewood Cliffs, NJ:
      Prentice-Hall, 1978.

641. Bundy, McGeorge. "Vietnam, Watergate, and
      Presidential Power." Foreign Affairs 58 (Winter
      1979): 397-407.

642. Cameron, Juan. "Richard Nixon's Very Personal White
      House." Fortune 82 (July 1970): 56-59+.

643. Chapel, Gage William. "Speech Writing in the Nixon
      Administration." Journal of Communication 26, 2
      (1976): 65-72.

644. Chesen, Eli S., and P.H. Wyden. President Nixon's
      Psychiatric Profile. New York, NY: David McKay,
      1974.

645. DeGregorio, William A. "Richard Nixon." The Complete
      Book of U.S. Presidents. New York, NY: December
      Books, 1984. pp. 580-601.

646. Dennis, Jack. "Who Supports the Presidency." Society
      13 (July/August 1976): 48-53.

647. Diamond, Robert A. Nixon: The Fourth Year of His
      Presidency. Washington, DC: Congressional
      Quarterly, Inc., 1973.

648. "Dick Nixon Show: Television Appearances Aid Nixon's
      Image." Nation 214 (January 24, 1972): 98-99.

649. Drury, Allen, and Fred Maroon. Courage and
      Hesitation. Garden City, NY: Doubleday, 1971.

650. Durbin, Louise. Inaugural Cavalcade. New York, NY:
      Dodd, Mead, 1971.

651. Ehrlichman, John. Witness to Power: The Nixon Years.
      New York, NY: Simon and Schuster, 1982.

652. Eisenhower, David. "Last Days in a Nixon White
      House." Good Housekeeping 181 (September 1975):
      89+.

653. Eisenhower, Julie Nixon. Eye on Nixon. New York, NY:
      Hawthorne Books, 1972.

654. Evans, Rowland, and Robert D. Novak. Nixon in the
      White House: the Frustration of Power. New
      York, NY: Random House, 1971.

655. "Four More Years." Commonweal 97 (December 1, 1972):
      195; 198-206+.

656. Gannon, Frank. "The Good Dog Richard Affair."
      American Spectator 14 (December 1981): 25-31.

657. Gartner, Alan. What Nixon Is Doing to Us. New York,
      NY: Harper and Row, 1973.

658. Goldbloom, Maurice J. "Nixon So Far." Commentary 49
      (February 1970): 29-38.

659. Graebner, Norman A. "Presidential Politics in a
      Divided America." Australian Journal of Politics
      and History 19 (April 1973): 28-47.

660. Harrington, Michael. "Anatomy of Nixonism." Dissent
      19 (Fall 1972): 563-578.

661. Harris, Michael. "Nixon: A Type to Remember." Nation
      219 (August 31, 1974): 134-137.

662. Harris, Richard. "Reflection on Nixon and Lincoln."
      New Yorker (April 5, 1974): 110.

663. Hartley, Anthony. "Nixon Regime." Encounter 32
      (March 1969): 20-24.

664. "Has the Press Done a Job on Nixon? The Fairness
      Problem Re-Examined." Columbia Journalism Review
      12 (January/February 1974): 50-58.

665. Henderson, Charles P. The Nixon Theology. New
      York, NY: Harper and Row, 1972.

666. Hersh, Seymour M. "Kissinger and Nixon in the White
      House." Atlantic 249 (May 1982): 35-53+.

667.   Hess, Allen K., and Dan Gossett. "Nixon and the
        Media: A Study of Non-Immediacy in Newspaper
        Editorials as Reflective of Geographical Attitude
        Differences." Psychological Report 34 (June 12,
        1974): 1055-1088.

668.   Higgins, George V. "Friends of Richard Nixon."
        Atlantic 234 (November 1974): 41-52.

669.   _____. The Friends of Richard Nixon. Boston, MA:
        Little, Brown and Company, 1975.

670.   "Highlights of Nixon Presidency, 1969-1974."
        Congressional Quarterly-Weekly Reports 32 (August
        10, 1974): 2092-2118.

671.   "Historians Rate Mr. Nixon." Newsweek 75 (January 26,
        1978): 14.

672.   Hoar, William P. "Presidential Autocities." American
        Opinion 20 (September 1977): 11-16+.

673.   Hoffman, Paul. The New Nixon. New York, NY: Tower
        Publications, 1970.

674.   Hoopes, Townsend. "President Is the Problem." New
        Republic 164 (March 6, 1971): 23-27.

675.   "How Nixon's White House Works." Time 95 (June 8,
        1970): 15-20.

676.   Howe, Irving. "And Now, God Help us, Nixon." Dissent
        16 (January/February 1969): 19-20.

677.   Jacobs, Richard f. "The Status of the Nixon
        Presidential Historical Materials." American
        Archivist 38, (July 1975): 337.

678.   Jenkins, Peter. "Portrait of a Presidency." New
        Statesman 87 (May 17, 1974): 688-692.

679.   Kaufer, David S. "Ironist and Hypocrite as
        Presidential Symbols: A Nixon-Kennedy Analog."
        Communication Quarterly 27 (Fall 1979): 20-26.

680.   Keefe, Robert. "On Cowboys and Collectives: The
        Kennedy-Nixon Generation." Massachusetts Review
        21, (Fall 1980): 551-560.

681. Kellermen, Barbara. "Introversion in the Oval
      Office." Presidential Studies Quarterly 13
      (Summer 1983): 383-399.

682. Keogh, James. President Nixon and the Press. New
      York, NY: Funk and Wagnalls, 1972.

683. Khan, Rais Ahmad. "The Nixon Administration--Problems
      and Prospects." Pakistan Horizon 22, 1 (1969):
      3-21.

684. Kilpatrick, James Jackson. "Report Card for Richard
      Nixon." National Review 21 (June 3, 1969): 532-
      537.

685. King, Andrew A., and Floyd D. Anderson. "Nixon, Agnew
      and the Silent Majority: A Case Study in the
      Rhetoric of Polarization." Western Speech 35
      (Fall 1971): 243-255.

686. Kingsbury, Roger. "Nixon Above the Storm Clouds."
      New Leader 52 (February 3, 1969): 3-5.

687. Kissinger, Henry. White House Years. Boston, MA:
      Little, Brown and Co., 1979.

688. _____. Years of Upheaval. Boston, MA: Little,
      Brown and Co., 1982.

689. Klein, Herbert. Making It Perfectly Clear. Garden
      City, NY: Doubleday, 1980.

690. Kraft, Joseph. "The Nixon Supremacy." Harpers 240
      (March 1970): 45-51.

691. Laing, Robert B., and Robert L. Stevenson. "Public
      Opinion Trends in the Last Days of the Nixon
      Administration." Journalism Quarterly 53 (Summer
      1976): 294-302.

692. Lashner, Marilyn A. The Chilling Effect in TV News:
      Intimidation by the Nixon White House. New York,
      NY: Praeger, 1984.

693. Lekachman, Robert. "Economics of Change." Commonweal
      95 (February 4, 1972): 419-420.

694. _____. "Nixon's Program." Commentary 47 (June
      1969): 67-72.

695. Lukas, J. Anthony. Nightmare: The Underside of the
     Nixon Years. New York, NY: Barnes and Noble,
     1976.

696. McDonald, Donald. "Two Years of the Nixon
     Administration." Center Magazine 4 (March/April
     1971): 21-28.

697. McGee, Gale A. "A Consitutional Crisis." Freedom at
     Issue 19, 1 (1973): 7-8; 21-23.

698. Mansfield, Michael Joseph. "Size-up of President
     Nixon." US News and World Report 71 (December 6,
     1971): 56-61.

699. Meyers, William. "Nixon's History Lesson: The Myth
     of Reprisals." Nation 209 (December 15, 1969):
     654-656.

700. Miller, Marvin (comp). The Breaking of a President.
     2 vols. Industry, CA: Therapy Productions,
     1974.

701. Mollenhoff, Clark R. Game Plan for Disaster: An
     Ombudsman's Report on the Nixon Years. New York,
     NY: W. W. Norton, 1976.

702. Morehead, Joe. "Into the Hopper: Tennis Elbow of the
     Soul: The Public Papers of Richard Nixon, 1973-
     1974." Serials Librarian 1 (Spring 1977): 207-
     214.

703. Morse, Wayne Lyman. "Supremacy and Secrecy." Nation
     216 (June 18, 1973): 777-779.

704. Nathan, Richard P. The Administrative Presidency.
     New York, NY: Wiley, 1983.

705. Neustadt, Richard E. Presidential Power: The
     Politics of Leadership with Reflections on Johnson
     and Nixon. New York, NY: John Wiley and Sons,
     1976.

706. Nixon, Richard M. A New Road for America: Major
     Policy Statements, March 1970 to October 1971.
     Garden City, NY: Doubleday and Company, 1972.

707. "The Nixon Administration and the News Media."
     Congressional Quarterly--Weekly Review 30 (January
     1, 1972): 3-7.

708. "Nixon After Six Months: Six Appraisals." <u>New York</u>
      <u>Times Magazine</u> (July 20, 1969): 4-5+.

709. "Nixon Interregnum." <u>New Republic</u> 169 (August 18,
      1973): 7-9.

710. <u>The Nixon Presidential Press Conference</u>. New York,
      NY: Earl M. Coleman Enterprises, Inc., 1978.

711. <u>Nixon: The First Year of His Presidency</u>. Washington,
      DC: Congressional Quarterly, 1970.

712. <u>Nixon: The Second Year of His Presidency</u>.
      Washington, DC: Congressional Quarterly, 1971.

713. <u>Nixon: The Third Year of His Presidency</u>. Washington,
      DC: Congressional Quarterly, 1972.

714. <u>Nixon: The Fourth Year of His Presidency</u>.
      Washington, DC: Congressional Quarterly, 1973.

715. <u>Nixon: The Fifth Year of His Presidency</u>. Washington,
      DC: Congressional Quarterly, 1974.

716. "Nixon's First Quarter: Assessment." <u>Time</u> 93 (April
      25, 1969): 19-20.

717. Osborne, John. "After Three Years." <u>New Republic</u> 166
      (January 15, 1972): 14-15.

718. _____. "Beach Party for the President: The Nixon
      Watch." <u>New Republic</u> 167 (September 1972): 21-
      24.

719. _____. <u>Fifth Year of the Nixon Watch</u>. New York,
      NY: Liveright Press, 1974.

720. _____. <u>Fourth Year of the Nixon Watch</u>. New York,
      NY: Liveright Press, 1973.

721. _____. <u>The Last Nixon Watch</u> New York, NY: E.P.
      Dutton, 1975.

722. _____. <u>The Nixon Watch</u>. New York, NY: Liveright
      Press, 1970.

723. _____. <u>Second Year of the Nixon Watch</u>. New York,
      NY: Liveright Press, 1971.

724. _____. <u>Third Year of the Nixon Watch</u>. New York,
      NY: Liveright Press, 1972.

725. _____. "Two Loners: R. Nixon and H. Kissinger."
     New Republic 168 (March 10, 1973): 13-15.

726. Padover, Saud K. "America's Imperial Presidency."
     Lithopinion 8 (Winter 1973): 34-44.

727. Paletz, David L., and Richard J. Umegar. "Presidents
     on Television: The Effects of Instant Analysis."
     Public Opinion Quarterly 41 (Winter 1977-1978):
     488-497.

728. Poirier, Richard. "Horatio Alger in the White House."
     Harper 245 (September 1972): 96.

729. Pomper, Gerald M. "Nixon and the End of Presidential
     Politics." Society 10 (March/April 1973): 14-16.

730. Price, Raymond. With Nixon. New York, NY: Viking
     Press, 1977.

731. Public Papers of the Presidents of the United States,
     Richard M. Nixon. 6 vols. Washington, DC: U.S.
     Government Printing Office, 1971-1975.

732. Rather, Dan, and Gary P. Gates. The Palace Guard.
     New York, NY: Harper and Row, 1974.

733. Raven, Bertram H. "The Nixon Group." Journal of
     Social Issues 30, 4 (1974): 297-320.

734. "Real Story of the Nixon Revolution." US News and
     World Report 70 (March 15, 1971): 29-34.

735. Reedy, George E. "The Omniscient President."
     Worldview 18 (July/August 1975): 10-14.

736. Reeves, Richard. "Beyond Re-election Day." Harper
     244 (April 1972): 54-56.

737. Reichley, A. James. "The Conservative Roots of the
     Nixon, Ford and Reagan Administrations."
     Political Science Quarterly 96 (Winter 1981/1982):
     537-550.

738. _____. Conservatives in an Age of Change: the
     Nixon and Ford Administration. Washington, DC:
     Brookings Institution, 1981.

739. "Richard M. Nixon: A Tenative Evaluation." Power and
      the Presidency. R.B. Semple. New York, NY:
      Charles Scribner and Sons, 1976. pp. 164-174.

740. "Richard Nixon's Mandate." Representative Men.
      Theodore L. Gross, New York, NY: Free Press,
      1970. pp. 50-58.

741. Roberts, David. "Who Rules Nixon." International
      Socialist Review 34, 10 (November 1973): 6-13.

742. Robinson, Donald L. "Presidential Autocracy and the
      Rule of Law." Current 151 (May 1973): 3-17.

743. Rosenberg, Leonard B. "Luck or Design: The Fall of
      Richard M. Nixon." Il Politico 40 (December
      1975): 706-709.

744. Safire, William. Before the Fall: An Inside View of
      the Pre-Watergate White House. New York, NY:
      Doubleday, 1975.

745. Schara, August W. "Richard M. Nixon." All the
      Presidents Plus Time and Biorhythms. Hicksville,
      NY: Exposition Press, 1978. pp. 151-159.

746. Schell, Jonathan. "Reflections: The Nixon Years."
      Pts. I-VI New Yorker (June 2, 9, 16, 30 and July
      7, 1975).

747. _____. The Time of Illusion. New York, NY:
      Alfred Knopf, 1976.

748. Schlesinger, Arthur M. The Imperial Presidency.
      Boston, MA: Houghton Mifflin, 1973.

749. _____. "Nixon and neo-Jeffersoniaism." The
      Seventies. Irving Howe and Michael Harrington.
      New York, NY: Harper and Row, 1972. pp. 421-423.

750. _____. "Runaway Presidency." Atlantic 232
      (November 1973): 43-55.

751. _____. "Skeptical Democrat Looks at President
      Nixon." New York Times Magazine (November 17,
      1968): 45-47+.

752. _____. "Who Wins a President's Paper?"
      Manuscripts 27 (Summer 1975): 178-182.

753. Schoenebaum, Eleanora. The Nixon/Ford Years. New
        York, NY: Facts on File, 1979.

754. "Second Term, Goals and Prospects." U.S. News and
        World Report 74 (January 1973): 15-16.

755. Semple, Robert B. "Nixon's Presidency Is A Very
        Private Affair." New York Times Magazine
        (November 2, 1969): 28-29+.

756. _____. "Richard M. Nixon: A Tentative
        Evaluation." Power and the Presidency. Philip C.
        Dolce and George H. Skau, eds. New York, NY:
        Scribners, 1976. pp. 164-174.

757. _____. "Three Strategies of a Master Politician."
        New York Times Magazine (November 1, 1970): 42.

758. Shawcross, William. "Tyrant in the White House." New
        Statesman 85 (January 19, 1973): 75-76.

759. Sorensen, Theodore C. "First Hundred Days of Richard
        M. Nixon." Saturday Review 52 (May 17, 1969):
        17-19.

760. Spear, Joseph C. Presidents and the Press: the Nixon
        Legacy. Cambridge, MA: MIT Press, 1984.

761. Spencer, Martin Z. "The Imperial Presidency and the
        Uses of Social Science." Midwest Quarterly 20
        (Spring 1979): 281-299.

762. Stein, Meyer L. "Nixon and Company." When Presidents
        Meet the Press. New York, NY: Messner, 1969.
        pp. 175-180.

763. Steinfels, Peter. "Man of the Year." Commonweal 95
        (January 21, 1972): 366.

764. Stillman, Edmund. "America After Vietnam."
        Commentary 52 (October 1971): 45-52.

765. "Summitry: From Peking to Moscow." Time 98 (October
        25, 1971): 10-12.

766. "Third Year: New Nixon on Economy, Foreign Affairs."
        Congressional Quarterly--Weekly Report 29
        (December 25, 1971): 2678-2683.

767. Vidal, Gore. "Nixon Without Knives." Fifty Who Made the Difference. New York, NY: Villard Books, 1984. pp. 28-33.

768. Vose, Clement R. "Nixon's Archival Legacy." PS 10 (Fall 1977): 432-439.

769. Watt, Donald C. "Four More Years--Of What?" Foreign Policy 9 (Winter 1973): 3-17.

770. Whalen, Richard J. "Republican White House: New Presidential Majority." Nation 215 (December 25, 1973): 648-651.

771. Wildavsky, Aaron. "The Past and Future Presidency." Political Theory 41 (Fall, 1975): 56-76.

772. "Will the Press Be Out to Get Nixon?" US News and World Report 65 (December 2, 1968): 39-40.

773. Wills, Garry. "Enigma of President Nixon." Saturday Evening Post 242 (January 25, 1969): 25-27+.

774. _____. "Richard Nixon, The Last Liberal." Washington Monthly 2 (October 1970): 23-33.

775. Witcover, Jules. "Salvaging the Presidential News Conference." Columbia Journalism Review 9 (Fall 1970): 27-34.

776. "With Lowered Voice, Enter Mr. Nixon." Newsweek 73 (February 3, 1969): 16-21.

Presidency - Domestic Affairs

Domestic issues never appeared to be a priority during the Nixon presidency. Richard Nixon was a moderate Republican politician who accepted the basic social revolution wrought by Franklin Rossevelt's New Deal. The guiding domestic philosophy of the Nixon presidency was to pare back some perceived excesses of Lyndon Johnson's Great Society legislation and maintain the status quo in domestic policy. Civil rights and minority population groups were the most affected by Nixon's domestic policies. Under the slogan of "new federalism," Richard Nixon instituted with Congressional approval a different approach to the distribution of federal money for social programs. This approach was labelled revenue sharing. Alen Mandell's article in a 1972 issue of Society, "Revenue Sharing: Game Plan or Trick Play?," is typical of the critics' analysis of Nixon's redistribution plan. Mandell refutes the Nixon administration claims that revenue sharing would better distribute federal money for social programs and create a more equal share for the various states in such distribution efforts. Rims Barber's and Joseph Huttie's article in a 1973 issue of New South, "Nixonian Economics: Another View," pointedly reveals the loss of federal social

programs effect on the impoverished black families in
Mississippi.

Civil rights in the late 1960s became entangled in the
question of busing to achieve school desegregation. The
issue was explosive as witnessed by the violence attendant
upon busing for desegregation court orders in Boston and
Pontiac, Michigan. The Nixon administration issued a
moratorium on future plans for busing to achieve school
desegregation. Constitutional considerations for this
moratorium were debated fiercely. Robert Bork's
Constitutionality of the President's Busing Proposals (1972)
argues the constitutional right of the Nixon
administration's action, but the moral right is still
debated. For many Americans involved in the civil rights
movement, the Nixon administration policies were a retreat
from civil rights gained in the mid-1960s. Leon Panetta's
and Pete Gall's Bring Us Together: The Nixon Team and Civil
Rights Retreat (1971) clearly labels the Nixon presidency as
anti-black. Ths indifference, according to Panetta and
Gall, stemmed from Nixon's view that black Americans were
not part of his electoral victory in 1968 and would not be
part of any future electoral voting. The busing issue for
the Nixon administration was political. This connection
between politics and the busing issue is argued convincingly
in Alexander Bickel's 1971 article for the New Republic.

Economics is a continuing domestic issue for all presidents. Richard Nixon, in very uncharacteristic Republican Party action, froze prices and wages and employed various manipulative economic policies in order to stimulate economic growth and stifle inflation. Nixon's actions in the economic area have been analyzed frequently. Rodney Morrison's Expectations and Inflation: Nixon, Politics, and Economics appeared in 1973. Neil DeMarchi wrote The First Nixon Administration: Prelude to Controls, in 1975 for the Brookings Institution. In 1981, Jon Frye and Robert J. Gordon wrote "Government Intervention in the Inflation Process: The Economics of Self-Inflicted Wounds" for the American Economic Review. The work of Roger Miller and Raburn Williams entitled The New Economics of Richard Nixon: Freezes, Floats, and Fiscal Policy (1972) labels Nixon's economic policies as revived old government manipulative actions that were done for political reasons alone.

One domestic issue was addressed early in the Nixon presidency, that of welfare reform. In 1969, Richard Nixon proposed a sweeping change in the welfare system's Aid to Dependent Children program. Though Nixon's proposal tied economic assistance to work opportunities for the needy, the proposal also guaranteed aid to all families with children that had income below a specified level. Joe Handler and Ellen Hollingsworth argued in their Stanford Law Review article "Work, Welfare, and the Nixon Reform Proposals"

(1970) that the Nixon proposals would actually increase the welfare rolls by 14 million people. Perhaps, because of the guaranteed income provision, some authors have lauded Nixon for this domestic policy initiative. Vincent Burke wrote Nixon's Good Deed: Welfare Reform in 1974. M. Kenneth Bowler published in 1974 The Nixon Guaranteed Income Proposal: Substance and Process in Policy Change, which was favorable to Nixon's approach. Both these works were preceded by the more scholarly Politics of a Guaranteed Income: the Nixon Administration and the Family Assistance Plan by Daniel Patrick Moynihan in 1973. This Nixon domestic policy proposal was rejected by the U.S. Senate and never implemented.

Reorganization of the executive branch bureaucracy was another Nixon administration domestic initiative that was rejected by the U.S. Congress. Richard Nathan's Plot That Failed: Nixon and the Administrative Presidency (1973) is an excellent review of the attempt by Nixon to restructure the federal bureaucracy within the executive branch. Nixon's plan would have placed presidential appointees directly in charge of entrenched segments of the bureaucracy in which both executive and legislative branch programs were frequently stalled or killed entirely. Nixon's proposal for executive branch reorganization has received considerable examination. Richard Cole and David Caputo wrote

"Presidential Years," for the <u>American Political Science Review</u> in 1979. Mohammed Khan wrote an article for a 1980 issue of <u>Political Science Review</u> entitled "Politics of Administrative Reorganization: President Nixon's Departmental Reorganization Program." In 1981, Jerel Rosati wrote for an issue of <u>World Politics</u> "Developing a Systematic Decision-Making Framework: Bureaucratic Politics in Perspective." The issue of executive branch reorganization was lost in the Watergate scandal that monopolized the federal government soon after Nixon's proposal. But, Douglas Fox pointed out in his article for <u>Public Administration Review</u> in 1973, "The President's Proposals for Executive Reorganization: A Critique," that Nixon's proposal was the most comprehensive plan for restructuring the federal bureaucracy ever submitted to a Congress of the United States.

777. Aberback, Joel D., and Bert Rockman. "Clashing Beliefs Within the Executive Branch: The Nixon Administration Bureaucracy." <u>American Political Science Review</u> 70 (June 1976): 456-468.

778. Ackerman, Frank, and Arthur MacEwan. "Inflation, Recession, and Crisis." <u>Radical America</u> 6, 1 (1972): 18-59.

779. Azevedo, Ross E. "Phase III--A Stabilization Program That Could Not Work." <u>Quarterly Review of Economics and Business</u> 16 (Spring 1976): 7-22.

780. Ball, Howard. <u>Controlling Regulatory Sprawl: Presidential Strategies from Nixon to Reagan</u>. Westport, CT: Greenwood Press, 1984.

781. Banfield, Edward C., et al. "Nixon, the Great
     Society, and the Future of Social Policy--A
     Symposium." Commentary 55 (May 1973): 31-61.

782. Barber, Rims, and Joseph J. Huttie. "Nixonian
     Economics: Another View." New South 28 (Spring
     1973): 72-78.

783. Beckler, David Z. "The Precarious Life of Science in
     the White House." Daedalus 103 (Summer 1974):
     115-134.

784. Bender, Robert. "Techniques of Subtle Erosion: R.
     Nixon's Supreme Court." Harper's 245 (December
     1972): 18+.

785. Bergsten, C. Fred. "The New Economics and U.S.
     Foreign Policy." Foreign Affairs 50 (January
     1972): 199-222.

786. Berman, Bruce J. "Richard Nixon and the New Corporate
     State." Queen's Quarterly 80 (Autumn 1973):
     425-433.

787. Bickel, Alexander M. "What's Wrong with Nixon's
     Busing Bill?" New Republic 165 (May 22, 1971):
     19-22.

788. Blackstock, Paul W. "The Intelligence Community Under
     the Nixon Administration." Armed Forces and
     Society 1 (February 1975): 231-250.

789. Bork, Robert H. Constitutionality of the President's
     Busing Proposals. Washington, DC: American
     Enterprise Institute for Policy Research, 1972.

790. Bowler, M. Kenneth. The Nixon Guaranteed Income
     Proposal: Substance and Process in Policy Change.
     Cambridge, MA: Ballinger Publishing Company,
     1974.

791. Brademas, John. "Revenue Sharing: The National
     Policy Debate." Publius 6 (Fall 1976): 155-159.

792. Brand, H. "Nixon and Social Immobilism." Dissent 16
     (May/June 1969): 209-213.

793. Buehler, John E. "The New Nixon Economic Plan: A
     Political Decision?" Arizona Review 20
     (August/September 1971): 1-4.

104

794. Burke, Vincent J. Nixon's Good Deed: Welfare Reform. New York, NY: Columbia University Press, 1974.

795. Calder, James D. "Presidents and Crime Control Kennedy, Johnson, and Nixon and the Influences of Ideology." Presidential Studies Quarterly 12 (Fall 1982): 574-589.

796. Clark, Gordon L. "The Spatial Division of Labor and Wage and Price Control of the Nixon Administration." Economic Geography 61 (April 1985): 113-128.

797. Clark, Kenneth B. "Eighteen Years After Brown." Integrated Education 10 (November/December 1972): 7-15.

798. Cole, Richard L., and David A. Caputo. "Presidential Control of the Senior Civil Service: Assessing the Strategies of the Nixon Years." American Political Science Review 73 (June 1979): 399-413.

799. Conlan, Timothy J. "The Politics of Federal Block Grants: from Nixon to Reagan." Political Science Quarterly 99 (Summer 1984): 247-270.

800. Coyne, Thomas J. "The Economic Impact of the Wage-Price Freeze." Akron Business and Economic Review 3 (Summer 1972): 20-26.

801. "Declaration of Independence: Can You Believe It? President Nixon May Turn Out To Be a Revolutionary Yet." Economist 238 (January 30, 1971): 39-40.

802. DeMarchi, Neil. "The First Nixon Administration: Prelude to Controls." Exhortation and Controls: The Search for a Wage-Price Policy, 1945-1971. Crawford D. Goodwin. Washington, DC: Brookings Institution, 1975.

803. "De-Vietnamization of America." Fortune 83 (May 1971): 133-134.

804. Doctors, Samuel I., and Anne S. Huff. Minority Enterprise and the President's Council. Cambridge, MA: Ballinger Publishers, 1973.

805. Dolbeare, Cushing N. "Nixon's Nonprogram for Housing." Dissent 21 (Winter 1974): 12-13.

806. Dowd, Douglas F. "King Richard's Political
     Arithmatic." New Politics 8 (Fall 1970): 4-12.

807. Dumbrell, John W., and John D. Less. "Presidential
     Pocket Veto Power: An Constitutional
     Anachronism?" Political Studies 28 (March 1980):
     109-116.

808. Dworkin, Ronald. "The Jurisprudence of Richard Nixon."
     New York Review of Books (May 4, 1972): 27-35.

809. Epstein, Edward. "The Krogh File: The Politics of
     Law and Order." Political Theory 39 (Spring
     1975): 99-124.

810. Evans, Lawrence, et al. "Phase III of Nixon's Anti-
     Union Drive." International Socialist Review 34
     (April 1973): 10-16.

811. Evans, Rowland, and Robert D. Novak. "Nixonomics:
     How the Game Plan Went Wrong." Atlantic 228 (July
     1971): 66-76+.

812. Fallows, James. "The Great Stagflation Machine."
     Washington Monthly 5 (October 1973): 53-60.

813. "First Americans: Indian Policy and the Environmental
     Protection Agency." Newsweek 76 (July 20, 1970):
     18.

814. Fisher, Louis. "Congress, The Executive, and the
     Budget." Annals of the American Academy of
     Political and Social Sciences 411 (January 1974):
     102-113.

815. Forbes, Jack D. Native Americans and Nixon:
     Presidential Politics and Minority Self-
     Determination 1969-1972. Los Angeles, CA:
     American Indian Studies Center, UCLA, 1981.

816. Fox, Douglas M. "The President's Proposals for
     Executive Reorganization: A Critique." Public
     Administration Review 33 (September/October 1973):
     401-406.

817. Freeman, Douglas N. "Freedom of Speech Within the
     Nixon Administration." Communication Quarterly 24
     (Winter 1976): 3-10.

818. Friendly, Fred W. "The Campaign to Politicize
      Broadcasting." Columbia Journalism Review 11
      (March/April 1973): 9-18.

819. Frye, Jon, and Robert J. Gordon. "Government
      Intervention in the Inflation Process: The
      Econometrics of Self-Inflicted Wounds." American
      Economic Review 71 (May 1981): 288-294.

820. "Galbraith Gives Nixon an A-minus: He Sees the Phase
      II Plan as an Endorsement of His Ideas About How
      the Economy Works." Business Week (October 16,
      1971): 74-76.

821. Gass, Oscar. "The Nixon Economy." Worldview 16 (July
      1973): 7-14.

822. Gerth, Jeff. "Nixon and the Mafia." Sundance
      (November/December 1972): 30-42.

823. Gillette, Robert. "Energy Crisis: President Sprints
      to Catch Up with Events." Science 182 (November
      23, 1973): 807-808.

824. _____. "White House Energy Policy: Who Has the
      Power?" Science 179 (March 23, 1973): 1211-1212.

825. Goetz, Charles J. What Is Revenue Sharing?
      Washington, DC: Urban Institute, 1972.

826. Goldberg, Arthur J. "The Administration's Anti-Busing
      Proposals--Politics Makes Loud Law." Northwestern
      University Law Review 67 (July/August 1972): 319-
      368.

827. Goldensohn, Richard. "The Dynamics of Inflation."
      Liberation 16 (June 1971): 16-21.

828. Gordon, Walter R. "Nixon Shifting Field." New Leader
      53 (May 25, 1970): 11-13.

829. Graham, Otis L. Toward a Planned Society: From
      Roosevelt to Nixon. New York, NY: Oxford
      University Press, 1976.

830. Graves, Thomas J. "IGR and the Executive Branch: the
      New Federalism." Annals of the American Academy
      of Political and Social Science. 416 (November
      1974): 40-51.

831. Hagoplan, Elaine. "Minority Rights in a Nation-State:
     The Nixon Administration's Campaign Against Arab-
     Americans." Journal of Palestine Studies 5,
     (Autumn 1975/Winter 1976): 97-114.

832. Hamilton, Mary T. "Price Controls in 1973:
     Strategies and Problems." American Economic
     Review 64 (May 1974): 100-104.

833. Handler, Joel F., and Ellen Jane Hollingsworth.
     "Work, Welfare, and the Nixon Reform Proposals."
     Stanford Law Review 22 (May 1970): 907-942.

834. Hart, John. "Executive Reorganization in the USA and
     the Growth of Presidential Power." Public
     Administration 52, (Summer 1974): 179-191.

835. Harvey, Mose L. "Preeminence in Space: Still a
     Central National Issue." Orbis 12 (Winter 1969):
     959-983.

836. Haskell, Gordon K. "Preventive Detention--Nixon's
     Baby." Dissent 16 (May/June 1969): 194-195.

837. Helco, Hugh. Government of Strangers: Executive
     Politics in Washington. Washington, DC:
     Brookings Institution, 1977.

838. Heller, Walter W. The Economy: Old Myth and New
     Realities. New York, NY: Norton, 1976.

839. Helmer, John, and Louis Maisel. "Analytical Problems
     in the Study of Presidential Advice: The Domestic
     Council in Flux." Presidential Studies Quarterly
     8, (Winter 1975): 45-67.

840. Hentoff, Nat. "Librarians and the First Amendment
     After Nixon." Wilson Library Bulletin 48,
     (September 1974): 724-741.

841. Hess, Stephen. "Richard Nixon, 1969-1974."
     Organizing the Presidency. Washington, DC:
     Brookings Institution, 1976. pp. 111-139.

842. Hoffman, Paul. "Nixon vs Rockefeller: The Politics
     of Abortion." Nation 214 (June 5, 1972): 712-
     713.

843. Hoffman, Wayne, and Ted Marmor. "The Politics of
     Public Assistance Reform: An Essay Review."
     Social Service Review 50, (March 1976), p. 11-22.

844. "Honing in on Domestic Programs." Business Week
        (August 16, 1969):   36-38; 100.

845. Howe, Irving. "Nixon's Dream--And Black Reality."
        Dissent 16 (March/April 1969):   101-107.

846. Hudson, William E. "The New Federalism Paradox."
        Policy Studies Journal 8 (Summer 1980):   900-906.

847. Huttie, Joseph J. "New Federalism and the Death of a
        Dream in Mound Bayou, Mississippi." New South 28,
        (Fall 1973):   20-29.

848. Johannes, John R. "From White House to Capitol Hill."
        Intellect 103 (March 1975):   356-360.

849. Johnson, Richard Tanner. "Nixon's Courtship with
        Crisis." Managing the White House. New York, NY:
        Harper and Row, 1974. pp. 199-229.

850. Kalven, Harry. "If This Be Asymmetry, Make the Most
        of It." Center Magazine 6 (May/June 1973):   36-
        37.

851. Karmin, Monroe W. "Nixon's Approach to Helping
        Blacks." Wall Street Journal 172 (December 9,
        1968):   20.

852. Kelly, David. "Mr. Nixon's Economics." Successo 10
        (November 1968):   51-55

853. Kessel, John H. The Domestic Presidency: Decision
        Making in the White House. Hemel Hempstead, UK:
        Duxbury Press, 1975.

854. Khan, Mohammad M. "Politics of Administrative
        Reorganization: President Nixon's Departmental
        Reorganization Program." Political Science Review
        19 (April/June 1980):   170-180.

855. Klumpp, James F., and Thomas A. Hollihan. "Debunking
        the Resignation of Earl Butz: Sacrificing an
        Official Racist." Quarterly Journal of Speech 65
        (February 1979):   1-11.

856. Land, F., and J. Ridgeway. "Health Economics."
        Ramparts Magazine 9 (June 1971):   6-7.

857. Lanzilloti, Robert F., and Blaine Roberts. "The
      Legacy of Phase II Price Controls." American
      Economic Review 64, (May 1974): 82-87.

858. Lekachman, Robert. "The New American Tories: A
      Critique of Nixon's Welfare Program." Dissent 16
      (November/December 1969): 471-476.

859. _____. "The Nixon Boom." New Leader 56 (February
      1973): 5-7.

860. _____. "Nixon's Program." Commentary 47 (June
      1969): 67-72.

861. Leiter, William M. "The Presidency and Non-Feudal
      Government: The Benefactor--Aversion Hypothesis,
      the Case of Public Assistance Policies in the New
      Deal and Nixon Administration." Presidential
      Studies Quarterly 10 (Fall 1980): 636-644.

862. Lessard, Suzannah. "Nixon and His Staff: The View
      from Their Own Mirror." Washington Monthly 4 (May
      1972): 53-59.

863. Levy, Leonard Williams. Against the Law: the Nixon
      Court and Criminal Justice. New York, NY: Harper
      and Row, 1974.

864. Lieberman, Carl. "President Nixon and Reorganization
      of the Executive Branch." Social Science 47
      (Autumn 1972): 195-202.

865. Long, F.A. "President Nixon's 1973 Reorganization
      Plan No. 1: Where Do Science and Technology Go?"
      Science and Public Affairs 29 (May 1973): 5-8,
      40-42.

866. McMahon, John F. "Revitalization of the National
      Security Council." Air University Review 21
      (March/April 1970): 28-36.

867. McMahon, Walter W. "Cooling Out the Economy."
      Transaction 8 (July/August 1971): 22-26.

868. McWilliams, Carey. "This Lawless Administration."
      Nation 215 (October 23, 1972): 354-356.

869. Malek, Frederic V. Washington's Hidden Tragedy: The
      Failure to Make Government Work. New York, NY:
      Free Press, 1978.

870. Madell, Allen S. "Revenue Sharing: Game Plan or Trick Play?" Society 9 (May 1972): 4,6,8.

871. Mars, David. "Nixon's New Federalism." Nation 210 (April 15, 1970): 435-437.

872. Masses, Benjamin L. "Nixon Plan for Reform of Taft-Hartley." America 120 (March 22, 1960): 322.

873. Mattick, Paul M. "Nixon's New Economic Policy." Radical America 6, 1 (1972): 4-17.

874. Miller, Roger L., and Raburn M. Williams. The New Economics of Richard Nixon: Freezes, Floats, and Fiscal Policy. New York, NY: Harper and Row, 1972.

875. Mills, Jon L., and William G. Munselle. "Unimpoundment: Politics and the Courts in the Release of Impounded Funds." Emory Law Journal 24 (Spring 1975): 313-353.

876. Mitchell, Daniel J.B. Wage-Price Controls and Labor Market Distortions. Washington, DC: Institute of Industrial Publications, 1976.

877. Moe, Ronald C. "Senate Confirmation of Executive Appointments: The Nixon Era." Proceedings of the Academy of Political Science 32, 1 (1975): 141-152.

878. Morrison, Rodney J. Expectations and Inflation; Nixon, Politics, and Economics. Lexington, MA: Lexington Books, 1973.

879. Morton, Rogers C. "The Nixon Administration Energy Policy." Annals of the American Academy of Political and Social Science 410 (November 1973): 65-74.

880. Moynihan, Daniel P. The Politics of a Guaranteed Income: The Nixon Administration and The Family Assistance Plan. New York, NY: Random House, 1973.

881. Mullaney, Thomas R. "A Populist in Nixon's Cabinet." New York Affairs 2, 4 (1975): 50-59.

882. Myers, Will S. "A Legislative History of Revenue
     Sharing." Annals of the American Academy of
     Political and Social Science 419 (May 1975): 1-
     11.

883. Nathan, Richard P. "The Administrative Presidency."
     Public Interest 44 (Summer 1974): 40-54.

884. _____. Plot That Failed: Nixon and the
     Administrative Presidency. New York, NY: John
     Wiley and Sons, 1975.

885. "New Federalism." Newsweek 74 (September 15, 1969):
     24-25.

886. "The Nixon Administration and Civil Rights, 1969-
     1970." Congressional Quarterly--Weekly Reports 28
     (November 27, 1970): 2853-2858.

887. "Nixon Backs Parochiaid: Voucher Parochiaid Plan
     Still Alive." Church and State 24 (October 1971):
     3+, 12-13.

888. "Nixon on Abortion." National Review 24 (May 26,
     1972): 570.

889. "Nixon Plan to Fight Hunger." US News and World
     Report 66 (May 19, 1969): 12.

890. "Nixon the Crime Fighter: Reckless Statement
     Regarding C. Manson." Nation 211 (August 17,
     1970): 98-99.

891. "Nixon, the Negro, and the Budget." Time 93 (April
     18, 1969): 19-20.

892. "Nixon to Tighten Airline Control." Aviation Week 90
     (March 3, 1969): 24-25.

893. "Nixon Way: School Desegregation." Newsweek 75
     (April 6, 1970): 28+.

894. "Nixon's New Plan to Run the Government: It's a Bold
     Nixon Stamp the President Is Now Determined to Put
     on the Government." U.S. News.

895. "Nixon's Share the Wealth Plan." Newsweek 77 (January
     18, 1971): 15-16.

896. Norton, Hughs. "Mr. Nixon's Economics: What Ever
     Happened to CEA (Council of Economic Advisors)."
     Business and Economics Review 19 (February 1973):
     2-8.

897. Osborne, John. "Nixon and the Blacks." New Republic
     159 (December 14, 1968): 19-20.

898. Otis, L. Graham. Toward a Planned Society: From
     Roosevelt to Nixon. Oxford, UK: Oxford
     University Press, 1976.

899. Panetta, Leon E., and Pete Gall. Bring Us Together:
     the Nixon Team and the Civil Rights Retreat.
     Philadelphia, PA: J.B. Lippincott, 1971.

900. "Picking Up the Wishbone: Anti-Inflation Measures."
     Time 95 (June 29, 1970): 10-11.

901. Polsby, Nelson W. "Presidential Cabinet Making:
     Lessons for the Political System." Political
     Science Quarterly 93 (Spring 1978): 15-25.

902. "Politics of Mr. Nixon's Economics." Life 68
     (February 13, 1970): 28.

903. Porter, William Earl. Assault on the Media: The
     Nixon Years. Ann Arbor, MI: University of
     Michigan Press, 1976.

904. "President Above the Law?" Economist 239 (April 10,
     1971): 47-48.

905. "President Nixon Outlines Proposals to Change
     Direction of Federal Spending." American City 88
     (April 1973): 114.

906. "President vs Congress." American 124 (March 20,
     1971): 279-280.

907. Randall, Ronald. "Presidential Power Versus
     Bureaucratic Intrasigence: The Influence of the
     Nixon Administration on Welfare Policy." American
     Political Science Review 73 (September 1979):
     795-810.

908. Raven, Bertram H. "The Nixon Group." Journal of
     Social Issues 30, 4 (1974): 297-320.

909. Reid, Frank. "Control and Decontrol of Wages in the
     United States: An Empirical Analysis." American

Economic Review 71 (March 1981): 108-120.

910. "Richard Nixon, Inflation Fighter." *Newsweek* 76
(December 14, 1970): 45-46.

911. Rinfret, Pierre A. "Nixon Economics: A Member of the
Nixon Economic Advisory Team Gives His View of
Life Under a New Administration." *Finance* 86
(November 1968): 12-14.

912. "The Road Nixon Is Taking on Civil Rights." *U.S. News
and World Report* 67 (July 21, 1969): 36-37.

913. Robins, Leonard. "The Plot That Succeeded."
Presidential Studies Quarterly 10 (Winter 1980):
99-106.

914. Rogers, William. "Nixon's Energy Policy: Exercise in
Political Duplicity." *Nation* 216 (May 1973):
646-650.

915. Rosati, Jerel A. "Developing a Systematic Decision-
Making Framework: Bureaucratic Politics in
Perspective." *World Politics* 33, 3 (January
1981): 234-252.

916. Rosen, George R. "The Consequences of Controls."
Dun's Review 115 (April 1980): 69-72.

917. Roucek, Irving S. "President Nixon's New Economic
Policy." *International Review of History and
Political Science* 9 (August 1972): 33-55.

918. Rourke, Frances E. "Executive Fallibility:
Presidential Management Styles." *Administration
and Society* 6 (August 1974): 171-177.

919. Runyon, Richard P., and Lawrence Rocks. "Lights Are
Going Out: Nixon's Energy Proposals." *National
Review* 25 (July 6, 1973): 728-730.

920. Schell, Jonathan. "Reflections: The Time of
Illusion." *New Yorker* 51 (June 2-July 7, 1975):
42-48+; 70-71+; 55-56+; 60-68; 39-44+; 38-48+.

921. Schiller, Brady. "Moving from Welfare to Workforce."
Public Policy 21 (Winter 1973); 125-133.

922. Schram, Sanford F. "Politics, Professionalism, and
the Changing Federalism." *Social Service Review*
55 (March 1981): 78-92.

923. Seidman, Harold. Politics, Position, and Power: The
     Dynamics of Federal Organization London, UK:
     Oxford, University Press, 1975.

924. Shani, Moshe. "US Federal Government Reorganization:
     Executive Branch Structure and Central Domestic
     Policy-Making Staff." Public Administration 52
     (Summer 1974): 193-208.

925. Sidey, H. "Nixon's Economic Bombshell." Life 71
     (August 27, 1971): 4; 20-25.

926. Silk, Leonard S. Nixonomics: How the Dismal Science
     of Free Enterprise Became the Black Art of
     Controls. New York, NY: Praeger, 1972.

927. Silvert, Freda. "The New Federalism and the New
     Corporatism." American Society of International
     Law Proceedings 68 (1974): 198-202.

928. Simon, James F. In His Own Image: The Supreme Court
     in Richard Nixon's America. New York, NY: David
     Mckay, 1973.

929. Stewart, Maxwell S. "Nixon's New Federalism: Is It
     the Answer?" Current History 61 (November 1971):
     279-283.

930. Strickland, Rennard, and Jack Gregory. "Nixon and the
     Indian." Commonweal 92 (September 4, 1970): 432-
     436.

931. Strong, Frank. "President, Congress, Courts: One Is
     More Equal Than Others." American Bar Association
     Journal 60 (September 1974): 1050-1052.

932. Szulc, Tad. "How Nixon Used the CIA." New York
     (January 1975).

933. Teeter, Dwight L. "Kicking Nixon Around Once More."
     Reviews in American History 4, 4 (1976): 607-613.

934. Vale, Vivian. "The Collaborative Chaos of Federal
     Administration." Government and Opposition 8
     (Spring 1973): 177-194.

935. _____. "The Obligation To Spend: Presidential
     Impoundment of Congressional Appropriations."
     Political Studies 25 (December 1977): 508-522.

936. Van Den Haag, E. "What's Missing in Nixon's Welfare
        Program?" National Review 22 (January 27, 1970):
        85-87+.

937. Waldman, Raymond J. "The Domestic Council:
        Innovation in Presidential Government." Public
        Administration 36 (May/June 1976): 260-268.

938. Walsh, John. "Drug Abuse Control: Policy Turns
        Toward Rehabilitation." Science 173 (July 2,
        1971): 32-34.

939. Weber, Arnold R. In Pursuit of Price Stabilty: The
        Wage Price Freeze of 1971. Washington, DC:
        Brookings Institution, 1973.

940. _____. "A Wage-Price Freeze as an Instrument of
        Income Policy: Or the Blizzard of 71." American
        Economic Review 62 (May 1972): 251-257.

941. White, Larry D. "Nixon's Push on the Marshmellow:
        Reorganization and Watergate, 1968-1974."
        Rendezvous 8 (Winter 1973-1974): 21-38.

942. Whitman, David. "Liberal Rhetoric and the Welfare
        Underclass." Society 21 (November/December 1983):
        63-69.

943. Wolk, Alan. The Presidency and Black Civil Rights,
        From Eisenhower to Nixon. Rutherford, NJ:
        Fairleigh Dickinson University Press, 1971.

944. Wollenberger, Joseph B. "Nixon v. Gissel: Shall the
        Twain Ever Meet?" Labor Law Journal 20 (December
        1969): 787-789.

945. Wolman, William. "The New Economics of Richard Nixon:
        A Radically Different Philosophy Will Be Brought
        to Bear on Economic, Fiscal, and Monetary
        Policies." Exchange 29 (December 1968): 1-7.

946. Zack, Allen Y. "Nixon's Credibility--The Economic
        Record." American Federationist 81 (February
        1974): 2-10.

Addresses, Speeches, and Statements

947. "Action for Progress (address on October 31, 1969)."
        Vital Speeches 36 (November 15, 1969): 70-73.

948. "Actions to Deal with the Menace of Air Piracy
      (statement on September 11, 1970)." Department of
      State Bulletin 63 (September 28, 1970): 342-353.

949. "Airline Hijacking (statement on September 11, 1970."
      Weekly Compilation of Presidential Documents 6
      (September 14, 1970): 1193-1194.

950. "All-Volunteer Armed Forced (statement on August 28,
      1972)." Weekly Compilation of Presidential
      Documents 8 (September 4, 1972): 1304.

951. "American Economy (radio address on February 21,
      1973)." Vital Speeches 39 (March 15, 1973): 322-
      323.

952. "The American Farmer (the president's address on
      nationwide radio, October 27, 1972)." Weekly
      Compilation of Presidential Documents 8 (October
      30, 1972): 1579-1581.

953. "The American Right of Privacy (the president's
      address on nationwide radio, February 23, 1974)."
      Weekly Compilation of Presidential Documents 10
      (February 25, 1974): 245-247.

954. "The American Veteran (the president's address on
      nationwide radio, October 22, 1972)." Weekly
      Compilation of Presidential Documents 8 (October
      39, 1972): 1551-1558.

955. "As Nixon Looks Beyond the Freeze (remarks on
      September 23, 1971)." US News and World Report 71
      (October 4, 1970): 77-79.

956. "Bombings and Bomb Threats (statement by the
      president, March 25, 1970)." Weekly Compilation
      of Presidential Document 6 (March 30, 1970): 442.

957. "Budget Revisions (statement by the president, May 19,
      1970)." Weekly Compilation of Presidential
      Documents 5 (May 25, 1970): 659.

958. "Call for Co-operation (excerpts from message to the
      Congress on September 11, 1970)." US News and
      World Report 69 (September 21, 1970): 71-73.

959. "Campaign Reform (the president's address on
      nationwide radio, March 8, 1974)." Weekly
      Compilation of Presidential Documents 7 (May 17,
      1971): 751-754.

960. "Campus Disorders (statement by the president, March
      22, 1969)." Weekly Compilation of President's
      Documents 5 (March 31, 1969): 458-459.

961. "Campus Revolutionaries: The Rights of Students
      (address on June 3, 1969)." Vital Speeches 35
      (July 1, 1969): 546-548.

962. "Cancer Cure Program (statement on May 11, 1971)."
      Weekly Compilation of Presidential Documents 7
      (May 17, 1971): 751-754.

963. "Challenges of the Third 100 Million (message to
      Congress on July 18, 1969)." US News and World
      Report 68 (January 12, 1970): 34.

964. "Chamber of Commerce of the United States (the
      president's remarks at Chamber's annual meeting,
      April 29, 1969) (Education)." Weekly Compilation
      of Presidential Documents 5 (May 5, 1969): 629-
      631.

965. "Combating Construction Inflation and Meeting Future
      Construction Needs (statement by the president,
      March 17, 1970)." Weekly Compilation of
      Presidential Documents 6 (March 23, 1970): 376-
      381.

966. "Commission on Obscenity and Pornography (statement on
      October 24, 1970)." Weekly Compilation of
      Presidential Documents 6 (November 2, 1970):
      1454-1456.

967. "Commission on Population Growth and the American
      Future (statement by the president June 4, 1970)."
      Weekly Compilation of Presidential Documents 6
      (June 8, 1970): 729-730.

968. "Communications Satellite Program (message to the
      Congress on February 26, 1970)." Department of
      State Bulletin 62 (April 20, 1970): 534.

969. "Community Development (radio address on March 4,
      1973)." Vital Speeches 39 (April 1, 1973): 356-
      357.

970. "Comprehensive Health Insurance Plan (the president's address on nationwide radio, May 20, 1974)." Weekly Compilation of Presidential Documents 10 (May 27, 1974): 532-534.

971. "Congressional Action and Government Spending (statement by the president, July 18, 1970)." Weekly Compilation of Presidential Documents 6 (July 20, 1970): 940-941.

972. "Consumer Product Information (statement on October 26, 1970)." Weekly Compilation of Presidential Documents 6 (November 2, 1970): 1459-1460.

973. "The Continuing Fight Against Inflation (the president's address to the nation, October 7, 1971)." Weekly Compilation of Presidential Documents 7 (October 11, 1971): 1375-1379.

974. "Crime and Drug Abuse (the president's address nationwide radio, October 15, 1972)." Weekly Compilation of Presidential Documents 8 (October 23, 1972): 1526-1528.

975. "Debt Ceiling and Social Security Benefits Increase (Statement on July 1, 1972)." Weekly Compilation of Presidential Documents 8 (July 3, 1972): 1122-1123.

976. "Depreciation Provisions of the Tax Laws (statement on January 11, 1971)." Weekly Compilation of Presidential Documents 7 (January 18, 1971): 58-59.

977. "Desegregation of America's Elementary and Secondary Schools (statement by the president, March 24, 1970)." Weekly Compilation of Presidential Documents 6 (March 30, 1970): 424-440.

978. "Drug Abuse Prevention and Control (remarks on June 17, 1971)." Weekly Compilation of Presidential Documents 7 (June 21, 1971): 930.

979. "Drugs and Defeatism (remarks on July 6, 1971)." US News and World Report 7 (July 19, 1971): 37.

980. "Economic Assistance and Investment Security in Developing Nations (the president's policy statement, January 19, 1972)." Weekly Compilation of Presidential Documents 8 (January 24, 1972): 64-66.

981. "Economic Plan (address on October 7, 1971)." Vital
      Speeches 38 (October 15, 1971): 2-4.

982. "Economic Policy and Productivity (the president's
      address to the nation June 17, 1970)." Weekly
      Compilation of Presidential Documents 6 (June 22,
      1970): 774-781.

983. "Educational and Busing (address on March 16, 1972)."
      Vital Speeches 38 (April 1, 1972): 354-355.

984. "Educational Opportunity and Busing (the president's
      address to the nation, March 16, 1972)." Weekly
      Compilation of Presidential Documents 8 (March 20,
      1972): 390-393.

985. "Energy and National Resources (statement by the
      president, June 29, 1973)." Weekly Compilation
      of Presidential Documents 9 (June 2, 1973): 867-
      874.

986. "Energy Emergency (address on November 7, 1973)."
      Vital Speeches 40 (December 1, 1973): 98-100.

987. "Environment: A National Mission for the Seventies."
      Fortune 81 (February 1970): 92.

988. "Equal Housing: Nixon Defines His Policy (excerpts
      from statement on June 11, 1971)." US News and
      World Report 70 (June 21, 1971): 72.

989. "Executive Order on Wages, Prices." US News and World
      Report 71 (August 30, 1971): 64-65.

990. "Executive Privilege (statement by the president,
      March 12, 1973)." Weekly Compilation of
      Presidential Documents 6 (March 19, 1973): 253-
      255.

991. "Federal Policies Relative to Equal Housing
      Opportunity (statement on June 11, 1971)." Weekly
      Compilation of Presidential Documents 6 (October
      26, 1970): 1434-1440.

992. "The Federal Responsibility to Education (address on
      October 25, 1972)." Weekly Compilation of
      Presidential Documents 8 (October 30, 1972): 1563-
      1565.

993. "Fighting Inflation is Everyone's Business (address on
      October 7, 1971)." Reader's Digest 99 (December
      1971): 77-80.

994. "Food, Nutrition, and Health (address on December 2,
      1969)." Vital Speeches 36 (June 1, 1970): 162-
      165.

995. "Four-front War on Poverty (address on August 8,
      1969)." Vital Speeches 35 (September 1, 1969):
      674-678.

996. "The Future of American Education (the president's
      address on nationwide radio, March 23, 1974)."
      Weekly Compilation of Presidential Documents 10
      (March 25, 1974): 351-352.

997. "The Future of the United States Space Program
      (statement by the president, March 7, 1970."
      Weekly Compilation of Presidential Documents 6
      (March 9, 1970): 328-331.

998. "Growing Menace of Drugs, Nixon's Plan to Fight It
      (message on July 14, 1969)." US News and World
      Report 67 (July 28, 1969): 60-62.

999. "Helping the Needy Go to College (message to the
      Congress on March 19, 1970)." American Education
      6 (May 1970): 28-31.

1000. "Housing Resouces (radio address on February 24,
      1973)." Vital Speeches 39 (March 15, 1973): 325-
      327.

1001. "Human Resources (radio address on February 24,
      1973)." Vital Speeches 39 (March 15, 1973): 325-
      327.

1002. "Industrial Design Classification Agreement (message
      to the Senate on August 3, 1971)." Department of
      State Bulletin 65 (August 30, 1971): 249.

1003. "Inflation (address on July 25, 1974)." Vital
      Speeches 40 (August 15, 1974): 644-648.

1004. "Inflation and Economic Policy (address on June 29,
      1970)." Vital Speeches 36 (July 1, 1970): 546-
      549.

1005. "Law Enforcement and Drug Abuse Prevention (radio address on March 10, 1973)." Vital Speeches 39 (April 1, 1973): 354-356.

1006. "Look to the Future (the president's address on nationwide radio and television, November 2, 1972)." Weekly Compilation of Presidential Documents 8 (November 6, 1973): 246-248.

1007. "Message on Education Reform." American Education 6 (April 1970): 30-34.

1008. "Minority Business Enterprise (statement by the prsident, March 5, 1969)." Weekly Compilation of Presidential Documents 5 (March 10, 1969): 371-373.

1009. "National Energy Policy (the president's address to the nation, November 25, 1973)." Weekly Compilation of Presidential Documents 9 (December 3, 1973): 1363-1366.

1010. "National Energy Situation (the president's nationwide radio address, January 19, 1974)." Weekly Compilation of Presidential Documents 10 (January 21, 1974): 64-66.

1011. "Nation's Economic Outlook (address on December 7, 1970)." Vital Speeches 37 (December 15, 1970): 130-133.

1012. "The Nation's Economy (the president's address on nationwide radio, May 25, 1974)." Weekly Compilation of Presidential Documents 10 (June 3, 1974): 549-551.

1013. "The Nation's Economy (the president's address to the nation, June 13, 1973)." Weekly Compilation of Presidential Documents 8 (June 18, 1973): 765-769.

1014. "The Nation's Economy (the president's radio address, July 1, 1973)." Weekly Compilation of Presidential Documents 9 (July 9, 1973): 879-881.

1015. "The Nation's Economy (statement by the president, September 28, 1972)." Weekly Compilation of Presidential Documents 8 (October 2, 1972): 1471-1472.

1016. "Nation's Needs as Nixon Sees Them (message to
       Congress on April 14, 1969)." US News and World
       Report 66 (April 28, 1969):L   324-325.

1017. "Natural Resources and the Environment (radio address
       on February 14, 1973)." Vital Speeches 39 (March
       15, 1973): 324-325.

1018. "The New Budget: Charting a New Era of Progress
       (president's address on nationwide radio)."
       Weekly Compilation of Presidential Documents 9
       (February 5, 1973): 84-86.

1019. "New Economic Policy (address on August 15, 1971)."
       Vital Speeches 37 (September 1, 1971): 674-676.

1020. "The 1970 Budget (statement by the president, July
       22, 1969)." Weekly Compilation of Presidential
       Documents 5 (July 28, 1969): 1020-1021.

1021. "Nixon Again Asks Congress for Private Pension Law
       Reform (excerpts from message to the Congress on
       April 11, 1973)." Aging` 223 (May 1973): 6.

1022. "Nixon Backs Space Future (excerpts from address)."
       Aviation Week 91 (December 1, 1969): 11.

1023. "Nixon in the Pulpit: Economic Evangelism (summary
       of address on September 6, 1971)." Time 98
       (September 20, 1971): 11-12.

1024. "Nixon: It Is My Duty (statement on ABM program
       March 14, 1969)." US News and World Report 66
       (March 24, 1969): 39-40.

1025. "Nixon on Message on Busing (March 17, 1972)." US
       News and World Report 72 (March 27, 1972): 70-
       74+.

1026. "Nixon Plan for Ending the Draft (message on April
       23, 1970)." US News and World Report 68 (May 4,
       1970): 25-27.

1027. "Nixon Steps Up His War on Inflation (address on
       October 17, 1969)." US News and World Report 67
       (October 27, 1969): 100-102.

1028. "Nixon: We Have An Obligation to the Next Generation
       (address on November 19, 1971)." US News and
       World Report 71 (December 6, 1971): 87-90.

1029. "Nixon: We Have to Put the Money Where the Problems Are (excerpts from address on September 1, 1969)." US News and World Report 67 (September 15, 1969): 82-84.

1030. "Nixon's Blueprint for War on Organized Crime (excerpts from message to Congress, April 23, 1969)." US News and World Report 66 (May 5, 1969): 43-44.

1031. "Nixon's Case for Tax Reform (excerpts from message on April 21, 1969)." US News and World Report 66 (May 5, 1969): 29.

1032. "Nixon's Desegregation (statement on March 24, 1970)." US News and World Report 68 (April 4, 1970): 80-87.

1033. "Nixon's Election Reform Plan (excerpts from radio address on May 16, 1973)." US News and World Report 74 (May 28, 1973): 105.

1034. "Nixon's Four-front War on Poverty (address on August 8, 1969)." Vital Speeches 35 (September 1, 1969): 674-678.

1035. "Nixon's Plea: Stop Making Heroes out of Criminals (excerpts from remarks on August 3, 1970)." US News and World Report 69 (August 17, 1970): 70.

1036. "Nixon's Views on Aid to Private Schools (address on April 6, 1972)." US News and World Report 72 (April 17, 1972): 97-98.

1037. "Nursing Homes (statement on August 6, 1971)." Weekly Compilation of Presidential Documents 7 (August 16, 1971): 1148-1150.

1038. "Offshore Oil Pollution (message to the Congress on May 20, 1970)." Department of State Bulletin 62 (June 15, 1970)." 754-756.

1039. "Older Americans: The President's (address on nationwide radio, October 30, 1972)." Weekly Compilation of Presidential Documents 8 (November 6, 1972): 1605-1607.

1040. "One America (address on October 28, 1972)." Weekly Compilation of Presidential Documents 8 (October 30, 1972): 1584-1586.

1041. "Only People Can Turn Back the Tide: Protecting
       Children Against Exposure to Erotic Publications
       (excerpts from message to Congress on May 2,
       1969)." US News and World Report 67 (July 21,
       1969): 53.

1042. "Phase IV of the Economic Stabilization Program
       (statement on July 18, 1973)." Weekly
       Compilation of Presidential Documents 9 (July 23,
       1973): 906-912.

1043. "Phase III of the Economic Stabilization Program
       (statement on May 28, 1973)." Weekly Compilation
       of Presidential Documents 9 (July 23, 1973):
       906-912.

1044. "The Philosophy of Government: (the president's
       address on nationwide radio, October 21, 1972)."
       Weekly Compilation of Presidential Documents 8
       (October 30, 1972): 1546-1548.

1045. "Planned Variation Program (statement by the
       president, July 29, 1971)." Weekly Compilation
       of Presidential Documents 7 (August 2, 1971):
       1094-1095.

1046. "President Calls for Comprehensive Drug Control
       Program (message to the Congress on June 17,
       1971)." Department of State Bulletin 65 (July
       12, 1971): 58-66.

1047. "President Nixon Continues To Seek Solution to
       Textile Problem (statement on March 11, 1971)."
       Department of State Bulletin 64 (April 5, 1971):
       490.

1048. "President Nixon: Intellectual Freedom in Danger
       (statement on March 23, 1969)." US News and
       World Report 66 (March 31, 1969): 30.

1049. "President Nixon Proposes Plan for Reorganization of
       Federal Drug Law Enforcement Activities (Message
       to the Congress on March 28, 1973)." Department
       of State Bulletin 68 (April 23, 1973): 498-502.

1050. "President Nixon: Rights of Majority Abused (message
       to Notre Dame on campus turmoil)." US News and
       World Report 66 (March 10, 1969): 11.

1051. "President Nixon's National Energy Policy (statement
       to the Congress on April 18, 1973)." Department
       of State Bulletin 68 (May 7, 1973): 561-566.

1052. "President Urges Nursing Home Reforms, Hints Action
       by U.S. (excerpts from address on June 25,
       1971)." Aging 201 (July 1971): 5+.

1053. "The President's Address to the Nation on Domestic
       Programs, August 8, 1969." Weekly Compilation of
       Presidential Documents 5 (August 11, 1969):
       1103-1112.

1054. "President's Blueprint for Meeting Nation's Needs
       (excerpts from message to the Congress on April
       18, 1973)." US News and World Report 74 (April
       30, 1973): 72-74+.

1055. "President's Message on Medical Care (excerpts from
       message to the Congress on February 18, 1971)."
       US News and World Report 70 (March 1, 1971): 70-
       74.

1056. "President's Message on Older Americans Proposes
       Strategy to Meet Their Problems." Aging 211 (May
       1972): 3+.

1057. "The President's Message to Congress on Equal
       Educational Opportunity." Current History 62,
       370 (1972): 305-311.

1058. "Price Freeze, Then Phase 4 (television address on
       June 13, 1973)." US News and World Report 74
       (June 25, 1973): 90-91.

1059. "Problems of Population Growth (message to the
       Congress on July 18, 1969)." Department of State
       Bulletin 61 (August 11, 1969): 105-111.

1060. "Protection and Enhancement of the Cultural
       Environment (statement by the president)."
       Weekly Compilation of Presidential Documents 7
       (May 17, 1971): 756-758.

1061. "Redirecting Executive Branch Management (statement
       on January 5, 1973)." Weekly Compilation of
       Presidential Documents 9 (January 8, 1973): 5-
       10.

1062. "Reform of Federal Criminal Laws (statement on
       January 16, 1971)." Weekly Compilation of
       Presidential Documents 7 (January 18, 1971): 68-
       69.

1063. "Reform of State Worker's Compensation Programs
       (statement by the president, May 15, 1974)."
       Weekly Compilation of Presidential Documents 10
       (May 20, 1974): 520-521.

1064. "Reform of the Federal Corrections System (statement
       by the president outlining 13 point program,
       November 13, 1969): 1592-1597.

1065. "Reforming the International Monetary System (remarks
       on September 25, 1972)." Department of State
       Bulletin 67 (October 23, 1972): 457-460.

1066. "Reorganizing White House (excerpts from message to
       the Congress)." US News and World Report 68
       (June 22, 1970): 80-81.

1067. "Rescuing the Environment (excerpt from message to
       the Congress on February 10, 1970)." US News and
       World Report 68 (February 23, 1970): 93-97.

1068. "Responsible University Leadership (address on
       September 16, 1970)." US News and World Report
       69 (September 28, 1970): 27-28.

1069. "Restructuring of Government Service Systems
       (statement by the president, March 27, 1969)."
       Weekly Compilation of Presidential Documents 5
       (March 31, 1969): 480-482.

1070. "Revenue Sharing (statement on October 20, 1972)."
       Weekly Compilation of Presidential Documents 8
       (October 23, 1972): 1534-1537.

1071. "Review of the 1970 Budget (statement of President,
       April 12, 1969)." Weekly Compilation of
       Presidential Documents 5 (April 21, 1969): 553-
       554.

1072. "The Rising Cost of Living (the president's address
       to the nation, October 17, 1969)." Weekly
       Compilation of Presidential Documents 5 (October
       20, 1969): 1427-1431.

1073. "Role of the Supreme Court (address on October 21, 1971)." US News and World Report 71 (November 1, 1971): 62-63.

1074. "A Salute to Agriculture: (the president's address on American agriculture, May 2, 1971)." Weekly Compilation of Presidential Documents 7 (May 10, 1971): 720-723.

1075. "Social Security and Welfare Reform (statement on May 18, 1971)." Weekly Compilation of Presidential Documents 8 (January 3, 1972): 775-776.

1076. "Social Security and Welfare Reform (statement on December 28, 1971)." Weekly Compilation of Presidential Documents 8 (January 3, 1972): 6-7.

1077. "Softwood Lumber and Plywood (statement by the president, June 9, 1970, on economic policy)." Weekly Compilation of Presidential Documents 6 (June 22, 1970): 787-790.

1078. "Space Shuttle Program (statement on January 5, 1972)." Weekly Compilation of Presidential Documents 8 (January 10, 1972): 27-28.

1079. "Strong Economy and a Strong National Defense (address on August 19, 1971)." Department of State Bulletin 65 (September 13, 1971): 273-276.

1080. "The Supersonic Transport Program (statement on December 5, 1970)." Weekly Compilation of Presidential Documents 6 (December 1970): 1630.

1081. "Tax Reform Act of 1969 (statement by the president, December 30, 1969)." Weekly Compilation of Presidential Documents 6 (January 5, 1970): 7-8.

1082. "Time for a Change (excerpts from message to the Congress on May 27, 1969)." US News and World Report 66 (June 9,1 1969): 44.

1083. "Trans-Alaskan Pipeline (statement on September 26, 1971)." Weekly Compilation of Presidential Documents 7 (October 4, 1971): 1349-1350.

1084. "Transportation Initiatives for the Nation (the president's address on nationwide radio, February 9, 1974)." Weekly Compilation of Presidential Documents 10 (February 18, 1974): 197-199.

1085. "26th Amendment to the Constitution (statement on July 5, 1971)." Weekly Compilation of Presidential Documents 7 (July 12, 1971): 1032-1034.

1086. "Urban Affairs (the president's address on nationwide radio, November 1, 1972)." Weekly Compilation of Presidential Documents 8 (November 6, 1972): 1608-1610.

1087. "Urban Mass Transportation Assistance Act of 1970 (statement on October 15, 1970)." Weekly Compilation of Presidential Documents 6 (October 19, 1970): 1375-1376.

1088. "Veterans' Affairs (the president's address on nationwide radio, March 31, 1974)." Weekly Compilation of Presidential Documents 10 (April 8, 1974): 378-379.

1089. "Veterans' Benefits Legislation (statement on October 24, 1972)." Weekly Compilation of Presidential Documents 8 (October 30, 1972): 1561-1562.

1090. "Voluntary Action (statement by the president, April 30, 1969)." Weekly Compilation of Presidential Documents 5 (May 5, 1969): 632-634.

1091. "Wage Price Freeze (message to the Congress on September 9, 1971)." Vital Speeches 34 (September 15, 1971): 706-709.

1092. "Wages and Prices in the Construction Industry (statement on March 29, 1971)." Weekly Compilation of Presidential Documents 7 (April 5, 1971): 581-588.

1093. "Water Quality Enforcement Program (statement on December 23, 1970)." Weekly Compilation of Presidential Documents 6 (December 28, 1970): 1724-1725.

1094. "We Are Not Democrats, or Republicans, We Are Americans (excerpts from address to House of Representatives on November 13, 1969)." US News and World Report 67 (November 24, 1969): 68.

1095. "Welfare Program (statement by the president, June 10, 1970)." Weekly Compilation of Presidential Documents 6 (June 15, 1970): 748-749.

1096.   "Welfare vs. Jobs (excerpts from address on April 19,
         1971)." US News and World Report 70 (May 3,
         1971): 67.

1097.   "When I Look at American Education (excerpts from
         statement on October 20, 1968)." Today's
         Education 58 (January 1969): 21-23.

1098.   "Wilderness Preservation (statement on April 28,
         1971)." Weekly Compilation of Presidential
         Documents 7 (May 3, 1971): 692-695.

Presidency--Foreign Affairs

When Richard Nixon became president in 1969, the most
urgent foreign policy issue was the continuing war in
Vietnam. During the election campaign, Nixon had indicated
that he had a secret plan to end the war in South Vietnam.
It took four years to accomplish that fact. Whatever the
truth about Nixon's secret plan campaign promise, as
president, Nixon moved to what he termed the
"Vietnamization" of the war. This concept involved the
gradual withdrawal of U.S. military forces from South
Vietnam while building the strength of the South Vietnamese
military forces so that they could fight the war without
U.S. military personnel. Robert Johnson, writing for
Foreign Affairs, "Vietnamization, Will It Work?" in 1970
carefully reviewed all possibilities for Nixon's
Vietnamization strategy and concluded it would not work.
During the course of the first two years as president,
Richard Nixon also lessened his reliance on Vietnamization
and broadened his strategy to end the war in Vietnam to
include a new foreign policy that differed sharply from that
of previous presidents.

Working with Henry Kissinger, who had taught Harvard
students that American domination of world events was no
longer possible, Nixon crafted a new direction and force for

U.S. foreign policy based upon a loss of American dominance
in world power and a need to approach potential world
problem areas with a consensus among the world's leading
nations about the appropriate course of action in order to
preserve peace. This concept has been commonly called
"detente" and has been compared historically with the
balance-of-power diplomacy of the nineteenth century.

The operation of this foreign policy during Nixon's
years as president is well documented in Ted Szulc's The
Illusion of Peace: Foreign Policy in the Nixon Years
(1978). Though somewhat critical of the Nixon foreign
policy concept, Szulc does not provide much analysis of the
policy's operation. Henry Brandon's Retreat of American
Power (1973) and Robert Osgood's Retreat from Empire (1973)
both provide analysis of Nixon's foreign policy in relation
to its actual operation on world events of the period. In
1976, Stephen Garret wrote "Nixonian Foreign Policy: A New
Balance of Power or a Revived Concert" for Polity. Garret
skillfully argues that Nixon's foreign policy was a revived
"concert" of powers similar to the "Concert of Europe"
following the Napoleonic wars and not a balance of power.
The Nixon Doctrine had renounced unilateral military
intervention. For Garret, the Nixon foreign policy can be
best understood when viewed as an effort to achieve a
coalition of world powers that act to protect the status quo
of world relations.

Most historians and political analysts have accepted
the fact that Nixon was refocusing American foreign policy
toward some balance of power among the US, USSR, and China.
But, Virginia Brodine and Mark Selden argue in their work
Open Secret: The Kissinger-Nixon Doctrine in Asia (1972)
that Nixon was not attempting to arrange a balance of power
among the world's nations but actually motivating other
world nations to police trouble spots while receiving their
instructions from Washington. Anthony Hartley's American
Foreign Policy in the Nixon Era (1975) takes a more
scholarly approach in its criticism of Nixon foreign policy.
Hartley lauds Nixon's acceptance of American non-dominance
of the world political structure but criticizes him for
failing to create a replacement structure. For Hartley, the
Nixon foreign policy created a network of overlapping
tactical moves that was in constant need of adjustment. The
system, according to Hartley, while easily manipulated by
Nixon and Kissinger, was not inheritable by future
presidents.

Whatever the real nature of Nixon's foreign policy as a
concept, the actual practice of the concept did produce the
Paris Accords of 1973 that ended the U.S. involvement in
South Vietnam. As early as 1972, J.L.S. Girling wrote
"Nixon's Algeria," for Pacific Affairs in which he argued
that some method to neutralize China was needed to win a

peaceful withdrawal of U.S. military forces from Vietnam.
This was the explanation advanced by Girling for Nixon's
visit to China. Jaya Baral's article in the 1975 issue of
International Studies, "Paris Talks on Vietnam and American
Diplomacy," clearly links Nixon's foreign policy concept
with efforts to neutralize the Soviet Union and China over
the issue of Vietnam in order to force a settlement at the
Paris talks. The actual sequence of events suggests that
Baral's article is very close to the real motivation for
detente and the balance of power concept encouraged by
Richard Nixon as president of the United States.

1099.   "Alert: President's Handling of First US Alert in
        Ten Years." Nation 217 (November 12, 1973):
        482-483.

1100.   "Alert That Wasn't Sounded: Overdue Energy Message."
        Fortune 87 (May 1973): 177.

1101.   Ambroz, Oton. "President Nixon's Trip to
        Yugoslavia." East Europe 20, 1 (1971): 16-18.

1102.   Aron, Raymond. "Richard Nixon and the Future of
        American Foreign Policy." Atlantic Community
        Quarterly 10 (Winter 1973): 473-445.

1103.   _____. "Richard Nixon and the Future of American
        Foreign Policy." Daedalus 101 (Fall 1972): 1-
        24.

1104.   Ball, Desmond. Deja Vu: The Return to Counter Force
        in the Nixon Administration Santa Monica, CA:
        California Seminar on Arms Control and Foreign
        Policy, 1975.

1105.   Ball, George W. Diplomacy for a Crowded World: An
        American Foreign Policy. Boston, MA: Little,
        Brown, and Company, 1976.

1106.   Baral, Jaya K.   "Paris Talks on Vietnam and American
        Diplomacy."   International Studies 14 (July
        1975): 375-395.

1107.   Binning, William C.   "The Nixon Foreign Policy for
        Latin America."   Inter-American Economic Affairs
        25 (Summer 1971): 31-45.

1108.   Brandon, Henry.   "Balance of Mutual Weaknesses:
        Nixon's Voyage into the World of the 1970s."
        Atlantic 231 (January 1973): 35-42.

1109.   _____. The Retreat of American Power. Garden
        City, NY: Doubleday, 1973.

1110.   Brenner, Michael J.   "The Problem of Innovation and
        the Nixon-Kissinger Foreign Policy."
        International Studies Quarterly 17 (September
        1973): 255-294.

1111.   Brodine, Virginia, and Mark Selden. Open Secret:
        The Kissinger-Nixon Doctrine in Asia. New York,
        NY: Harper and Row, 1972.

1112.   Brown, Seyom. The Crises of Power: An
        Interpretation of United States Foreign Policy
        During the Kissinger Years. New York, NY:
        Columbia University Press, 1979.

1113.   Brzezinski, Zbigniew.   "The Deceptive Structure of
        Peace."   Foreign Policy 14 (Spring 1974): 35-55.

1114.   _____.   "The State of Nixon's World (1): Half
        Past Nixon."   Foreign Policy 3 (Summer 1971): 3-
        21.

1115.   _____.   "U.S. Foreign Policy: The Search for
        Focus."   Foreign Affairs 51 (July 1973): 707-
        727.

1116.   Buchan, Alastair.   "A World Restored?"   Foreign
        Affairs 50 (July 1972): 644-659.

1117.   Bundy, McGeorge.   "Vietnam, Watergate, and
        Presidential Powers."   Foreign Affairs 58 (Winter
        1979-1980): 397-407.

1118.   Bundy, William P.   "The Nixon Policies in Asia and
        the Pacific."   Pacific Community 2 (October
        1970): 77-86.

1119. Burchett, Wilfred. "The Nixon Plan and Indochina
       Realities." _International Affairs_ 1 (January
       1970): 45-48.

1120. Burke, John P. "Responsibilities of Presidents and
       Advisers: A Theory and Case Study of Vietnam
       Decision Making." _Journal of Politics_ 46
       (August 1984): 818-845.

1121. Buss, Claude Albert. _China: The People's Republic
       of China and Richard Nixon_. San Francisco, CA:
       W.H. Freeman and Company, 1974.

1122. Butwell, Richard. "The Nixon Doctrine in Southeast
       Asia." _Current History_ 61 (December 1971): 321-
       326.

1123. Chancellor, John. "Who Produced the China Show."
       Foreign Policy 7 (Summer 1972): 88-92.

1124. "China Policy: Nixon Moves Cautiously to Modify
       China Policy." _Congressional Quarterly-Weekly
       Report_ 28 (February 20, 1970): 578-584.

1125. Clough, Ralph N. "Musing on Nixon's Peking Visit."
       Foreign Policy 4 (Fall 1971): 130-137.

1126. Cohen, Samuel T. "Whatever Happened to the Nixon
       Doctrine?" _Policy Review_ 26 (Fall 1983): 88-92.

1127. _Congress Speaks on Nixon's Visit to Mainland China_.
       Washington, DC: Capital Publishers, 1972.

1128. Deakin, James. "Who Is Making US Foreign Policy:
       The New or the Old Nixon?" _War/Peace Report_ 10
       (December 1970): 3-7.

1129. DeFronzo, John. "Nixon's Visit to China and
       Increased Favorability Toward Communism."
       Psychological Reports 42 (February 1978): 70.

1130. Destler, I.M. "The Nixon NSC (2): Can One Man Do?"
       Foreign Policy 5 (Winter 1971-1972): 28-40.

1131. _____. "The Nixon System: A Further Look."
       Foreign Service Journal 51 (February 1974): 28-
       29.

1132. Draper, Theodore. "Detente." _Commentary_ 57 (June
       1974): 25-47.

1133.   Duff, Peggy. "The Paris Accords." Journal of
        Contemporary Asia 3, 2 (1973): 204-211.

1134.   Dutt, Gargi. "China and The Shift in Superpower
        Relations." International Studies 13 (October
        1974): 635-662.

1135.   English, H.E. "Nixon's Economic Opportunities."
        International Journal 24 (Spring 1969): 310-326.

1136.   Gaddis, John Lewis. "The Rise, Fall, and Future of
        Detente." Foreign Affairs 62 (Winter 1983/1984):
        354-377.

1137.   Galbraith, John Kenneth. "Decline of American
        Power." Equire 77 (March 1972): 79-84+.

1138.   Gardner, Lloyd C. The Great Nixon Turnaround,
        America's New Foreign Policy in the Post-Liberal
        Era. New York, NY: New Viewpoints, 1973.

1139.   Garfinkle, Adam. "The Nixon Diplomatic Initatives:
        An Evaluation." Orbis 17 (Winter 1974): 1414-
        1420.

1140.   Garret, Stephan A. "Nixonian Foreign Policy: A New
        Balance of Power or a Revived Concert." Polity 8
        (Spring 1976): 389-421.

1141.   Garthoff, Raymond L. Detente and Confrontation:
        American-Soviet Relations from Nixon to Reagan.
        Washington, DC: Brookings Institution, 1985.

1142.   Gelb, Leshe H. "The Essential Domino: American
        Politics and Vietnam." Foreign Affairs 50 (April
        1972): 459-475.

1143.   Geyelin, Philip. "Impeachment and Foreign Policy."
        Foreign Policy 15 (Summer 1974): 183-190.

1144.   Gilbert, Stephen P. "Implications of the Nixon
        Doctrine for Military Aid Policy." Orbis 16
        (Fall 1972): 660-681.

1145.   Girling, J.L.S. "Nixon's Algeria--Doctrine and
        Disengagement in Indochina." Pacific Affairs 44
        (Winter 1971/1972): 527-544.

1146.   Glabinski, Stanislaw. President Nixon's 24 Hours in
        Warsaw. Warsaw, Poland: Interpress, 1972.

1147. Grant, James P. "President Nixon's Strange Dilemma and His Unprecedented Opportunity." International Development Review 11 (March 1969): 23-24.

1148. Gutpa, Vinod. Anderson Papers: A Study of Nixon's Blackmail of India. Columbia, SC: South Asia Books, 1972.

1149. Hahn, Walter F. "The Nixon Doctrine: Design and Dilemmas." Orbis 16 (Summer 1972): 361-376.

1150. Halberstam, David. "President Nixon and Vietnam." Harper 238 (January 1969): 22+.

1151. Harrington, Michael. "Anatomy of Nixonism: Or the Miracle Kissinger Wrought." Dissent 19 (Fall 1972): 563-578.

1152. Hartley, Anthony. American Foreign Policy in the Nixon Era. London, UK: International Institute for Strategic Studies, 1975.

1153. _____. "The U.S., the Arabs, and Israel." Commentary 49 (March 1970): 45-50.

1154. Hassner, Pierre. "The State of Nixon's World (3): Pragmatic Conservatism in the White House." Foreign Policy 3 (Summer 1971): 41-61.

1155. Hecht, James L. "Quest for Community: Mixed Housing in the Suburbs." Nation 214 (March 6, 1972): 305-308.

1156. Hersh, Seymour M. "Kissinger and Nixon in the White House." Atlantic 249 (May 1982): 35-68.

1157. Hoadley, J. Stephen. "Coalition Building in South Vietnam: A Critique." Asian Forum 3, 1 (1971): 67-68.

1158. Hoffman, Stanley. "Will It Balance at Home?" Foreign Policy 7 (Summer 1972): 60-86.

1159. Hon, Richard D. Nixon's Peking Trip--The Road to China's Russian War. San Francisco, CA: Henson Company, 1972.

1160. Hughes, Thomas L. "Is Nixon a Foreign Policy Problem?" Current 1159 (February 1974): 3-11.

1161. Hunter, Robert E. "The ABM: President Nixon's Safeguard Programmer." World Today 35 (May 1969): 194-202.

1162. "The Impact of the Nixon Ceausecu Meeting." East Europe 18 (August/September 1969): 33-35.

1163. "Initiative Lost in a Cloud of Communications." Economist 236 (July 11, 1970): 39-40.

1164. Johnson, Robert H. "Vietnamization: Will It Work?" Foreign Affairs 48 (July 1970): 629-647.

1165. Jones, Alan M. US Foreign Policy in a Changing World: The Nixon Administration--1969-1973. New York, NY: David McKay, 1973.

1166. Jones, Donald K. "Commitment, Disengagement, and the Nixon Doctrine." Military Review 53, 12 (1973): 27-38.

1167. Kahin, George M. "Nixon's Peace Plan: No Basis for Negotiation." New Republic 166 (February 12, 1972): 12-14.

1168. Kaltefleiter, Werner. "Europe and the Nixon Doctrine: A German Point of View." Orbis 17 (Spring 1973): 75-94.

1169. Kaplan, Lawrence S. "NATO and the Nixon Doctrine: Ten Years Later." Orbis 24 (Spring 1980): 149-164.

1170. Kaplan, Morton A. The Nixon Initiative and Chinese-American Relations. Edwardsville, IL: Southern Illinois University Press, 1972.

1171. Karnow, Stanley. "Mr. Nixon's Return Engagement in Cambodia." New Republic 168 (April 28, 1973): 15-17.

1172. Kattenburg, Paul M. "The Nixon New Look in Foreign Policy." World Affairs 135 (Fall 1972): 115-128.

1173. Kennedy, Edward M. "Beyond Detente." Foreign Policy 16 (Fall 1974): 3-29.

1174. Kerr, Malcolm H. "Nixon's Second Term: Policy Prospects in the Middle East." Journal of Palestine Studies 2 (Spring 1973): 14-29.

1175. Kintner, William R. The Impact of President Nixon's Visit To Peking on International Politics. Philadelphia, PA: Foreign Policy Research Institute, 1972.

1176. Kissinger, Henry, et al. "Forging a New Foreign Policy." Current 142 (July/August 1972): 51-64.

1177. Kobayashi, Katsumi. The Nixon Doctrine and US-Japanese Security Relations. Santa Monica, CA: California Seminar on Arms Control and Foreign Policy, 1975.

1178. Kohl, Wilfred L. "The Nixon-Kissinger Foreign Policy System and U.S.-European Relations: Patterns of Policy Making." World Politics 28 (October 1975): 1-43.

1179. Kolko, Gabriel. "Nixon's Vietnam Strategy." Commonweal 98 (March 1973): 55-59.

1180. Kolodziej, Edward A. "Congress and Foreign Policy: The Nixon Years." Proceedings of the Academy of Political Science 32, 1 (1975): 167-179.

1181. _____. "Foreign Policy and the Politics of Interdependence: The Nixon Presidency." Policy 9 (Winter 1976): 121-157.

1182. Laird, Melvin R., et al. The Nixon Doctrine. Washington, DC: American Enterprise Institute for Public Policy Research, 1972.

1183. _____. "A Strong Start in a Difficult Decade: Defense Policy in the Nixon Years." International Security 20 (Fall, 1985): 5-26.

1184. Leacacos, John P. "The Nixon NSC (1): Kissinger's Apparent." Foreign Policy 5 (Winter 1971-1972): 3-27.

1185. Lehman, John F. The Executive, Congress, and Foreign Policy: Studies in Interorganizational Relations. New York, NY: Praeger, 1976.

1186. "Lessons of Vietnam." Monthly Review 37 (June 1985): 1-13.

1187. Levin, N. Gordon. "Nixon, the Senate, and the War."
       Commentary 50 (October 1970): 69-84.

1188. Litwak, Robert S. Detente and the Nixon Doctrine.
       New York, NY: Cambridge University Press, 1984.

1189. MacFarquhar, Roderick. "Nixon's China Pilgrimage."
       World Today 28 (April 1972): 153-161.

1190. McLennan, Barbara N. "Implications of the Nixon
       Doctrine for American International
       Negotiations." Il Politico 39 (December 1974):
       553-566.

1191. Manning, Clarence A. "President Nixon and American
       Policy." Ukrainian Quarterly 25 (Spring 1969):
       67-74.

1192. Maruyama, Shizuo. "The Nixon Doctrine and Ping-Pong
       Diplomacy." Japan Quarterly 18 (July-September
       1971): 266-272.

1193. Medick, Monika. "The Nixon New Economic Policy:
       Economic and Security Interests in US-European
       Relations." American Studies 21, 1 (1978): 73-
       89.

1194. Meselon, Matthew S. "Behind the Nixon Policy for
       Chemical and Biological Warfare." Bulletin of
       the Atomic Scientists 25 (December 1969): 23-34.

1195. Michael, Franz. "The New United States-China
       Policy." Current History 63 (September 1972):
       126-129.

1196. "Mr. Nixon's Philosophy of Foreign Policy." Round
       Table 248 (October 1972): 403-410.

1197. "Mr. Nixon's Trip to Moscow." New Republic 170 (May
       4, 1974): 5-6.

1198. Moll, Kenneth L. "Realistic Deterence and New
       Strategy." Air University Review 23, 1 (1971):
       2-12.

1199. "Moscow Summit--Why? Goals of the Nixon Trip." US
       News and World Report 72 (May 29, 1972): 28-31.

1200. Nathan, James A. "Commitments in Search of Roost."
       Virginia Quarterly Review 50, (Summer, 1974):
       322-347.

1201. Neal, Fred Warner, and Mary K. Harvey. *Pacem in
       Terris III* vol. 1: The Nixon-Kissinger Foreign
       Policy: Opportunities and Contradictions. Santa
       Barbara, CA: Center for the Study of Democratic
       Institutions, 1974.

1202. Neruda, Pablo. *A Call for the Destruction of Nixon
       and Praise for the Chilean Revolution*.
       Cambridge, MA: West End Press, 1980.

1203. Nicholas, H.G. "The Nixon Line." *Yearbook of World
       Affairs*. London, UK: Stevens, 1974. pp. 15-25.

1204. "Nixon Doctrine: Analysis of Foreign Policy
       Message." *New Republic* 162 (February 28, 1970):
       5-6.

1205. "Nixon on Castro." *Inter-American Economic Affairs*
       25 (Spring 1972): 81-82.

1206. "Nixon's Coup: To Peking for Peace." *Time* 98 (July
       26, 1971): 11-12+.

1207. "Nixon's Goal: Dealing from Strength." *Business
       Week* (November 9, 1968): 100-103.

1208. "Nixon's Peace Plan." *New Republic* 163 (October 17,
       1970): 5-6.

1209. Nizami, Taufig Ahmad. "Richard Nixon and Peking."
       Indian Journal of Politics 6 (January-June 1972):
       123-127.

1210. "No Time to Lose." *Atlantic Community Quarterly* 18
       (Winter 1980-1981): 436-449.

1211. "Now Just Watch Me: The New Nixon Era for
       International Relations." *Economist* 34 (February
       21, 1970): 15-16; 45-46.

1212. Olsen, Edward A. "The Nixon Doctrine in East Asian
       Perspective." *Asian Forum* 5 (January/March
       1973): 17-28.

1213. Osborne, John. "Respite with Brezhnev." *New
       Republic* 168 (June 30, 1973): 12-14.

1214. _____. "Sunshine Summitry." New Republic 168 (April 14, 1973): 11-13.

1215. Osgood, Robert E., et al. Retreat from Empire: The First Nixon Administration Baltimore, MD: Johns Hopkins University Press, 1973.

1216. Overholt, William H. "President Nixon's Trip to China and Its Consequences." Asia Survey 13 (July 1973): 707-721.

1217. Parker, Maynard. "Vietnam: The War That Won't End." Foreign Affairs 53 (January 1975): 352-374.

1218. Parrent, Allan. "International Affairs in the Nixon Administration: His Lack of Commitment to Specific Programs Could Be an Asset." Christianity and Crises 28 (January 20, 1969): 343-346.

1219. Patcher, Henry. "Detente--Reality and Myth." Dissent 21 (Winter 1974): 21-29.

1220. _____. "The Nixon Regime and Foreign Policy." Dissent 16 (January/February 1969): 25-27.

1221. Paterson, Thomas G. "After Peking, Moscow: New Levers of Containment." Nation 214 (April 24, 1972): 531-532.

1222. Pauker, Guy J., et al. In Search of Self-Reliance: US Security Assistance to the Third World Under the Nixon Doctrine. Santa Monica, CA: The Rand Corporation, 1973.

1223. Peretz, Dan. "The United States, the Arabs, and Israel: Peace Efforts of Kennedy, Johnson, and Nixon." Annals of the Academy of Political and Social Science 401 (May 1972): 116-125.

1224. Pike, David W. Latin America in Nixon's Second Term. Paris, France: American College in Paris, 1982.

1225. Pipes, Richard. "America, Russia, and Europe in the Light of the Nixon Doctrine." Survey 19 (Summer 1973): 30-40.

1226. Ploss, Sidney. "Soviet-American Relations: Hope and Anxiety." Russian Review 31 (July 1972): 216-225.

1227. "Policy and Performance: Foreign Policy Message."
New Republic 164 (March 6, 1971): 5-6.

1228. "Politics of the Event: Nixon's Visit to China."
Nation 214 (March 6, 1972): 292-293.

1229. Poole, Peter A. The United States and Indochina,
From FDR to Nixon. Hinsdale, IL: Dryden Press,
1973.

1230. Porter, D. Gareth. "Vietnam: Politics of the Paris
Agreement." Current History 65 (December 1973):
247-251.

1231. "President Nixon's China Initiative: A Conference
Report." Orbis 15 (Winter 1972): 1206-1212.

1232. "President Nixon's Visit to China." Current Notes on
International Affairs 43, 2 (1972): 48-54.

1233. Pye, Lucian W. "China and the United States: A New
Phase." Annals of the American Academy of
Political and Social Science 402 (July 1972):
97-106.

1234. "Quarterback's Peace." Commonweal 95 (February 11,
1972): 435-436.

1235. Ravenall, Earl C. "The Nixon Doctrine and Our Asian
Commitments." Foreign Affairs 49 (January 1971):
201-207.

1236. _____. "Secrecy, Consensus, and Foreign Policy:
The Logic of Choice." Townson State Journal of
International Affairs 10, 1 (1975): 1-12.

1237. _____. "The States of Nixon's World (2): The
Political Military Gap." Foreign Policy 3
(Summer 1971): 22-40.

1238. Reeves, Richard. "Nixon's Secret Strategy." Harper
243 (December 1971): 96-98.

1239. Richardson, Elliot L. "The Foreign Policy of the
Nixon Administration: Its Aims and Strategy."
Department of State Bulletin 61 (September 22,
1969): 257-260.

1240. Richardson, William J. "President Nixon's China
Trip." America 125 (August 21, 1971): 84-87.

1241. Roberts, Chalmers M. "Foreign Policy under a
       Paralyzed Presidency." Foreign Affairs 52 (July
       1974): 675-689.

1242. Rosenfeld, Stephen S. "Nixon Faces Mid-East Again."
       Present Tense 1, 1 (1973): 5-8.

1243. Rowe, David N. "The Nixon China Policy and the
       Balance of Power." Issues and Studies 9 (May
       1973): 12-28.

1244. "Rumania: President Nixon's Visit and the Tenth
       Party Congress." World Today 25 (September
       1969): 369-370.

1245. Rush, Kenneth. "The Nixon Administration Foreign
       Policy Objectives." Department of State
       Bulletin 68 (April 23, 1973): 476-483.

1246. Schurmann, Franz. The Foreign Policies of Richard
       Nixon: The Grand Design. Berkeley, CA:
       Institute of International Studies, University of
       California, 1986.

1247. Scoville, Herbert. "Flexible Madness." Foreign
       Policy 14 (Spring 1974): 164-177.

1248. SerVaas, Barbara. "Russia: 1974 Style." Saturday
       Evening Post 246 (November 1974): 57-63+.

1249. Shawcross, William. Sideshow: Kissinger, Nixon, and
       the Destruction of Cambodia. New York, NY:
       Simon and Schuster, 1979.

1250. Sherman, Michael E. "Nixon and Arms Control."
       International Journal 24 (Spring 1969): 327-
       328.

1251. Shih-fu, Lo. "Detente and the Fall of Vietnam and
       Cambodia." Issues and Studies 11 (July 1975):
       30-38.

1252. Simon, Sheldon W. "The Nixon Doctrine and Prospects
       for Asian Regional Security Cooperation." Asian
       Forum 5 (January/March 1973): 1-16.

1253. Simpson, Stanley. "Assessing the Nixissinger
       Diplomacy." Current 160 (March 1974): 56-60.

1254. Sloan, John W. "Three Views of Latin America: President Nixon, Governor Rockefeller, and the Latin American Consensus of Vina del Mar." Orbis 14 (Winter 1971): 934-950.

1255. Smith, Russell H. "The Presidential Decision in the Cambodian Operation: A Case Study in Crisis Management." Air University Review 22, 6 (1971): 45-53.

1256. Sorley, Lewis. Arms Transfer Under Nixon: A Policy Analysis. Lexington, KY: University of Kentucky Press, 1983.

1257. Starr, Harvey. "The Kissinger Years--Studying Individuals and Foreign Policy." International Studies Quarterly 24 (December 1980): 465-496.

1258. Stathes, Stephen. "Nixon, Watergate, and American Foreign Policy." Presidential Studies Quarterly 13 (Winter 1983): 129-147.

1259. Stevens, Robert Warren. Vain Hopes, Grim Realities: The Economic Consequences of the Vietnam War. London, UK: Croom Helm, 1976.

1260. Sulzberger, Cyrus L. The World of Richard Nixon. Englewood Cliffs, NJ: Prentice-Hall, 1987.

1261. Summers, Laura. "Cambodia: Model of the Nixon Doctrine." Current History 65 (December 1973): 252-256; 276.

1262. Sylvester, Anthony. "President Nixon's Visit to Bucharest." East Europe 18 (August/September 1969): 4-5.

1263. Szulc, Tad. The Illusion of Peace: Foreign Policy in the Nixon Years. New York, NY: Viking Press, 1978.

1264. Taylor, Trevor. "President Nixon's Arm Supply Policies." Yearbook of World Affairs. London, UK: Stevens, 1977, pp. 65-80.

1265. Thomson, J.C. "Will the Nixon Administration Recognize Communist China." Pacific Community 2 (October 1970): 97-100.

1266. Tsou, Tang. "Statesmanship and Scholarship." World Politics 26 (April 1974): 428-451.

146

1267. Van Der Linden, Frank. Nixon's Quest for Peace. New York, NY: David McKay, 1972.

1268. Van Hollen, Christopher. "The Tilt Policy Revisited: Nixon-Kissinger Geopolitics in South Asia." Asian Survey 20 (April 1980): 339-361.

1269. Vartabedian, Robert A. "Nixon's Vietnam Rhetoric: A Case Study of Apologia as Generic Paradox." Southern Speech Communication Journal 50 (Summer 1985): 366-381.

1270. "Vietnam: The Nixon Plan." Newsweek 73 (May 26, 1969): 33-36.

1271. Volsky, Daniel. "Behind the Nixon Plan." New Times 6 (February 1972): 4-5.

1272. Walerstein, Immanuel. "From Nixon to Nixon." African Report 14 (November 1969): 28-30.

1273. Warner, Edwin. "Richard Nixon: An American Disraeli?" Time 100 (November 27, 1972): 18-19.

1274. Watt, David. "Kissinger's Track Back." Foreign Policy 37 (Winter 1979-80): 59-66.

1275. Weinstein, Allen. "The Symbolism of Subversion: Notes on Some Cold War Icons." Journal of American Studies 6 (August 1972): 165-179.

1276. We-ming, Sung. "Nixon Doctrine in America's Asian Policy." Asian Outlook 5 (May 1970): 15-17.

1277. "What Is Nixon's Policy?" National Review 21 (February 25, 1969): 158+.

1278. Whiting, Allen S. "Sino-American Detente." China Quarterly 82 (June 1980): 334-341.

1279. Whitney, David C. Quest for a Lasting Peace: President Richard Nixon's Historic Visit to Austria, USSR, Iran, and Poland, May 20-June 1, 1972. Chicago, IL: JG Ferguson Publishing Company, 1972.

1280. _____. The Week That Changed the World: President Richard M. Nixon's Historic Visit to Communist China. Chicago, IL: JG Ferguson Publishing Company, 1972.

1281. Wildavsky, Aaron. "Was Nixon Tough? Dilemmas of American State Craft." Society 16 (November 1978): 25-35.

1282. Wilhelm, Alfred D. "Nixon Shocks and Japan." Military Review 54, 11 (1974): 70-77.

1283. Wilson, Richard, ed. The President's Trip to China: A Pictorial Record of the Historic Journey to the Peoples Republic of China. New York, NY: Bantam Books, 1978.

1284. Wood, Robert Jefferson. "Military Assistance and the Nixon Doctrine." Orbis 15 (Spring 1971): 247-274.

1285. Wormuth, Francis D. "The Nixon Theory of the War Power: A Critique." California Law Review 60 (May 1972): 623-704.

Speeches

1286. "Address to the People of the Soviet Union (May 28, 1972)." Vital Speeches 38 (August 15, 1972): 649-650.

1287. "Address to the People of the Soviet Union (address on July 2, 1974)." Vital Speeches 40 (August 1, 1974): 610-612.

1288. "Agreement with Japan on Reversion of Okinawa (message to Senate on September 21, 1971)." Department of State Bulletin 65 (October 18, 1971): 431-433.

1289. "Amendment to U.S.-U.K. Atomic Energy Agreement (message to the Congress on January 26, 1970)." Department of State Bulletin 62 (March 16, 1970): 361.

1290. "America in the World City (address to National Industrial Conference Board, September 12, 1967." Conference Board Record 4 (October 1967): 2-6.

1291. "American Strength: The Keystone of Peace (address on May 29, 1971)." Department of State Bulletin 64 (June 28, 1971): 813-815.

1292. "America's Role in the World (address on June 4,
          1969)." Vital Speeches 35 (July 1, 1969): 548-
          550.

1293. "Balance of Payments (statement by the president,
          April 4, 1969)." Weekly Compilation of
          Presidential Documents 5 (April 7, 1969): 507-
          510.

1294. "Ballistic Missile Defense System (statement by
          president, March 14, 1969)." Weekly Compilation
          of Presidential Documents 5 (March 17, 1969):
          406-409.

1295. "Broadcasting Agreements with Mexico (message to
          Senate on March 15, 1969). Department of State
          Bulletin 60 (April 14, 1969): 330.

1296. "The Cambodian Sanctuary Operation (the president's
          interim report to the nation, June 3, 1970)."
          Weekly Compilation of Presidential Documents 5
          (June 8, 1970): 728-725.

1297. "Cambodia Strike: Defensive Action for Peace
          (address on April 30, 1970)." Department of
          State Bulletin 62 (May 18, 1970): 617-621.

1298. "The Challenge of Peace (the president's radio and
          television address to the nation, August 15,
          1971)." Weekly Compilation of the Presidential
          Documents 7 (August 23, 1971): 1168-1172.

1299. "Chemical and Biological Defense Policies and
          Programs (statement on November 25, 1969)."
          Department of State Bulletin 61 (December 15,
          1969): 541-543.

1300. "Continuation of Radio Free Europe and Radio Liberty
          (statement on March 11, 1972)." Department of
          State Bulletin 66 (April 10, 1972): 544.

1301. "Continuing US Efforts on Behalf of Prisoners of War
          and Missing in Southeast Asia (remarks on
          September 28, 1971)." Department of State
          Bulletin 65 (October 25, 1971): 357-358+.

1302. "Convention on Biological and Toxin Weapons (message
          to the Senate on August 10, 1972)." Department
          of State Bulletin 67 (September 4, 1972): 253.

1303. "Convention on Terrorism (message to the Senate on
       May 11, 1971)." Department of State Bulletin 65
       (July 5, 1971): 28.

1304. "Defending the Defenders (summary of address at US
       Air Force Academy)." Time 93 (June 13, 1969):
       15.

1305. "Denying Hanoi: The Means to Continue Aggression
       (address on May 9, 1972): Department of State
       Bulletin 66 (May 29, 1972): 747-750.

1306. "Easing Trade and Travel Restrictions on China
       (statement on April 14, 1971)." Current History
       6 (September 1971): 178-179+.

1307. "Economic Assistance and Investment Security in
       Developing Nations (statements on January 19,
       1972)." Weekly Compilations of Presidential
       Documents 8 (January 24, 1972): 64-66.

1308. "Ending the War and Vesting the Peace (address on
       January 23, 1973)." Vitals Speeches 39
       (February 15, 1973): 268-269.

1309. "Establishment of Peace (address to U.N. on September
       18, 1969)." Vital Speeches 35 (October 1, 1969):
       738-741.

1310. "Executive Privilege (statement on March 12, 1973)."
       Weekly Compilation of Presidential Documents 9
       (March 19, 1973): 253-255.

1311. "Facing the Facts in Vietnam (address on January 26,
       1965)." Vital Speeches 31 (March 15, 1965):
       337-340.

1312. "First Step Toward Peace (excerpt from television
       address on January 17, 1974)." US News and World
       Report 76 (January 28, 1974): 26.

1313. "Food for Peace Report for 1968 (message to Congress
       on April 22, 1969)." Department of State
       Bulletin 60 (June 23, 1969): 547.

1314. "Foreign Aid Program for Fiscal Year 1970: New
       Directions in Foreign Aid (message to Congress on
       May 28, 1969)." Department of State Bulletin 60
       (June 16, 1969): 515-519.

1315. "Foreign Assistance for the Seventies (message to the Congress on September 15, 1970)." Department of State Bulletin 62 (October 5, 1970): 369-378.

1316. "Foreign Policy (the president's address on nationwide radio, November 4, 1972)." Weekly Compilation of Presidential Documents 8 (November 13, 1972): 1639-1641.

1317. "General Assembly of the United Nations (the president's address, September 18, 1969)." Weekly Compilation of Presidential Documents 5 (September 22, 1969): 1275-1282.

1318. "Geneva Protocol on Gases and Bacteriological Warfare (message to the Senate on August 9, 1970)." Department of State Bulletin 63 (September 7, 1970): 273.

1319. "In the President's Words: What US Is Doing in Laos (statement on March 6, 1970)." US News and World Report 68 (March 16, 1970): 86-88.

1320. "Indochina: An Equitable Proposal for Peace (address on January 25, 1972)." Department of State Bulletin 66 (February 15, 1972): 181-185.

1321. "Indochina Progress Report: An Assessment of Vietnamization (address on April 7, 1971)." Department of State Bulletin 64 (April 26, 1971): 537-540.

1322. "International Aspects of Environmental Quality (message on August 7, 1972)." Department of State Bulletin 67 (September 18, 1972): 308-313.

1323. "International Aspects of the 1971 Environment Program (excerpts from message on February 8, 1971)." Department of State Bulletin 64 (March 1, 1971): 253-256.

1324. "International Aspects of the 1972 Environmental Program (excerpts from message on February 8, 1972)." Department of State Bulletin (March 6, 1972): 301-303.

1325. "International Monetary Fund and World Bank (address on September 25, 1972)." Vital Speeches 39 (October 15, 1972): 2-4.

1326. "Internationl Wheat Agreement, 1971 (message to the
          Senate)." Department of State Bulletin 65 (July
          12, 1971): 66.

1327. "Let Us Forge an Alliance (excerpts from address on
          January 14, 1971)." US News and World Report 70
          (January 25, 1971): 44.

1328. "Meaning of Midway (statement on June 10, 1969)." US
          News and World Report 66 (June 23, 1969): 29.

1329. "Meeting Our Responsibilities Abroad (excerpts from
          remarks made November 9, 1971)." Department of
          State Bulletin 65 (November 29, 1971): 613-614.

1330. "Moscow: Address to the People of the Soviet Union
          (the president's radio and television address,
          May 28, 1972)." Weekly Compilation of
          Presidential Documents 8 (January 5, 1972): 939-
          942.

1331. "Moscow Summit: New Opportunities in US-Soviet
          Relations (address on June 1, 1972)." Department
          of State Bulletin 66 (June 26, 1972): 855-859.

1332. "Moving Forward on the Agenda of Peace (address on
          November 4, 1972)." Department of State Bulletin
          67 (November 27, 1972): 624-627.

1333. "New Approach to Pan American Problems (remarks on
          April 14, 1969)." Department of State Bulletin
          60 (May 5, 1969): 384-386.

1334. "The New Initiative for Peace in Southeast Asia (the
          president's radio and television address to the
          nation, October 7, 1970)." Weekly Compilation of
          Presidential Documents 6 (October 12, 1970):
          1349-1352.

1335. "New Peace Initiative for All Indochina (address on
          October 7, 1970)." Department of State Bulletin
          63 (October 26, 1970): 465-467.

1336. "1971: A Year of Break-Throughs Toward Peace in the
          World (address on February 9, 1972)." Department
          of State Bulletin 66 (March 6, 1972): 289-291.

1337. "Nixon: Time Has Come to End This War (statement on
          September 16, 1969)." US News and World Report
          67 (September 29, 1969): 32.

1338. "Patent and Copyright Conventions (message to the
       Senate on March 12, 1969)." Department of State
       Bulletin 60 (April 7, 1969): 298.

1339. "Peace in perspective (excerpts from remarks on
       February 1, 1973)." Department of State Bulletin
       68 (February 19, 1973): 196-197.

1340. "Peaceful Competition (address on October 23, 1970)."
       Vital Speeches 37 (November 15, 1970): 66-69.

1341. "People's Republic of China (statement by the
       president April 14, 1971)." Weekly Compilation
       of Presidential Documents 7 (April 19, 1971):
       628-629.

1342. "The People's Republic of China (the president's
       radio and television address to the nation, July
       15, 1971)." Weekly Compilation of Presidential
       Documents 7 (July 19, 1971): 1058.

1343. "A Plan for Peace in Vietnam (the president's address
       to the nation, January 25, 1972)." Weekly
       Compilation of Presidential Documents 8 (January
       31, 1972): 120-125.

1344. "Pragmatism and Moral Force in American Foreign
       Policy (address on June 5, 1974)." Department of
       State Bulletin 71 (July 1, 1974): 1-5.

1345. "President Affirms U.S. Cooperation in World Economic
       Affairs (remarks on September 29, 1971)."
       Department of State Bulletin 65 (October 25,
       1971): 450-452.

1346. "President Announces Major Step in SALT Negotiations
       (statement on May 20, 1971)." Department of
       State Bulletin 64 (June 7, 1971): 741-742.

1347. "President Asks Senate Approval of Protocol II to
       Treaty for the Prohibition of Nuclear Weapons in
       Latin America (message on August 13, 1970)."
       Department of State Bulletin 63 (September 14,
       1970): 305.

1348. "President Explains His Risks for Peace (remarks on
       December 15, 1969)." US News and World Report 67
       (December 29, 1969): 15-16.

1349. President Nixon Approves Policy Statement on
       International Air Transportation (statement on
       June 22, 1970)." Department of State Bulletin 63
       (July 20, 1970): 86.

1350. "President Nixon Calls for Comprehensive Efforts in
       Multilateral Disarmament Negotiations (message on
       July 3, 1969)." Department of State Bulletin 61
       (July 28, 1969): 65-66.

1351. "President Nixon Discusses Background and Purpose of
       His Visit to the Soviet Union (remarks on May 19,
       1972)." Department of State Bulletin 66 (June
       12, 1972): 803-807.

1352. "President Nixon Discusses 1969 Decision To Bomb
       Cambodia (excerpt from address on August 20,
       1973)." Department of State Bulletin 69
       (September 10, 1973): 341-345.

1353. "President Nixon Discusses Reaction to Peace
       Initiative (remarks on October 8, 1970)."
       Department of State Bulletin 63 (October 26,
       1970): 467-470.

1354. "President Discusses Responsibility for Decision on
       Vietnam Policy (message)." Department of State
       Bulletin 61 (November 3, 1960): 371.

1355. "President Nixon Discusses the Objectives of His
       European Trip (excerpts from message on February
       21, 1969)." Department of State Bulletin 60
       (March 17, 1969): 217-219.

1356. "President Nixon Hails Saigon Proposals for Political
       Settlement in South Vietnam (statement on July
       11, 1969)." Department of State Bulletin 61
       (July 28, 1969): 61-62.

1357. "President Nixon Reduces Troop Ceiling in Vietnam
       (statement on September 16, 1969)." Department
       of State Bulletin 61 (October 6, 1969): 302.

1358. "President Nixon Reiterates Policy on Withdrawal from
       Indochina (statement on November 17, 1971)."
       Department of State Bulletin 65 (December 6,
       1971): 658.

1359. "President Nixon Urges Senate Action on Nuclear
        Nonproliferation Treaty (message to the Senate on
        February 5, 1969)." Department of State Bulletin
        60 (February 24, 1969): 162.

1360. "President Nixon's Veto of War Powers Measure
        Overriden by the Congress (message to the
        Congress on October 24, 1973)." Department of
        State Bulletin 69 (November 26, 1973): 662-664.

1361. "President Nixon's White Paper on Cambodia (statement
        on June 30, 1970)." US News and World Report 69
        (July 13, 1970): 81-86.

1362. "President Pays Tribute to Captives and Missing in
        Southeast Asia (statement on March 13, 1971)."
        Department of State Bulletin 64 (April 5, 1971):
        489.

1363. "President Pledges Continued Efforts on Behalf of
        POWs and MIAs (remarks on October 16, 1972)."
        Department of State Bulletin 67 (November 6,
        1972): 532-533.

1364. "President Pledges Rededication of US Support for the
        UN (statement on January 9, 1970)." Department
        of State Bulletin 62 (March 16, 1970): 358.

1365. "President Reaffirms Importance of Inter-American
        System (remarks on April 13, 1973)." Department
        of State Bulletin 68 (May 28, 1973): 686-687.

1366. "President Reaffirms U.S. Support of European
        Community (statement of October 27, 1972)."
        Department of State Bulletin 67 (November 20,
        1972): 608.

1367. "President Reports on the War in Cambodia (address on
        June 3, 1970)." U.S. News and World Report 68
        (June 15, 1970): 77-79.

1368. "President Requests Additional Funds for South Asian
        Relief (statement of October 1, 1974)."
        Department of State Bulletin 65 (October 25,
        1971): 444.

1369. "President Welcomes South Vietnam's Initiative on
        Prisoners of War (statement on April 14, 1971)."
        Department of State Bulletin 64 (May 3, 1971):
        568.

1370.   "President's Message to Congress on Trade (excerpts
        from message to the Congress on April 10, 1973)."
        US News and World Report 74 (April 23, 1973):
        89-92.

1371.   "Progress Report on Our Plan for Peace in Vietnam
        (address on December 15, 1969)." Department of
        State Bulletin 62 (January 5, 1970): 1-3.

1372.   "Purpose of America's Power (address on March 12,
        1971)." Department of State Bulletin 64 (April
        5, 1971): 487-489.

1373.   "Quality of Like in the Americas (statement)."
        Department of State Bulletin 61 (December 8,
        1969): 493-494.

1374.   "Redefinition of the United States Role in the World
        (address on February 25, 1971)." Department of
        State Bulletin 65 (March 15, 1971): 305-310.

1375.   "Reform of the US Foreign Assistance Program (message
        to the congress on April 21, 1971)." Department
        of State Bulletin 64 (May 10, 1971): 614-625.

1376.   "Report on Progress in Vietnam (address on April 20,
        1970)." Department of State Bulletin 62 (May 11,
        1970): 65-74.

1377.   "A Report on the Conclusion of the Cambodian
        Operation." Department of State Bulletin 6, 3
        (July 20, 1970): 65-74.

1378.   "Report on the Situation in Southeast Asia (The
        President's address to the nation, April 7,
        1971)." Weekly Compilation of Presidential
        Documents 7 (April 12, 1971): 611-616.

1379.   "Report on Vietnam (the president's report to the
        nation, December 14, 1969)." Weekly Compilation
        of Presidential Documents 5 (December 22, 1969):
        1752-1755.

1380.   "Report on Vietnam (the president's report to the
        nation, April 20, 1970)." Weekly Compilation of
        Presidential Documents 6 (April 27, 1970): 53-
        57.

1381.   "Report on Vietnam (the president's address to the
        nation, April 26, 1972)." Weekly Compilation of
        Presidential Documents 8 (May 1, 1972): 790-794.

1382. "Report to the Nation on Summit (address on July 3, 1974)." Vital Speeches 40 (August 1, 1974): 612-614.

1383. "Role of National Defense in Our Efforts for Peace (address on August 24, 1972)." Department of State Bulletin 67 (September 25, 1972): 344-348.

1384. "Search for Genuine Place is a Still-Perilous World (excerpts from statement on US foreign policy for the 1970s on May 3, 1973)." US News and World Report 74 (May 14, 1973): 102-104.

1385. "Settlement That Will Accomplish Our Basic Objectives in Vietnam (excerpts from address on November 2, 1972)." Department of State Bulletin 67 (November 20, 1972): 605-606.

1386. "The Situation in Laos (statement by the president, March 6, 1970)." Weekly Compilation of Presidential Documents 6 (March 9, 1970): 322-328.

1387. "The Situation in Southeast Asia (the president's address to the nation, April 30, 1970)." Weekly Compilation of Presidential Documents 6 (May 4, 1970): 596-601.

1388. "The Situation in Southeast Asia (the president's address to the nation, May 8, 1972)." Weekly Compilation of Presidential Documents 6 (May 4, 1970): 596-601.

1389. "Situation in Vietnam (address April 26, 1972)." Vital Speeches 38 (May 15, 1972): 450-452.

1390. "Sound Limitations on Armaments Urged by President Nixon (message on February 23, 1971)." Department of State Bulletin 64 (March 15, 1971): 310-311.

1391. "Strategic Arms Limitation Talks (statement on May 20, 1971)." Weekly Compilation of Presidential Documents 7 (May 24, 1971): 783-784.

1392. "Strong Economy and a Strong National Defense (address on August 19, 1971)." Department of State Bulletin 65 (September 13, 1971): 273-276.

1393. "Top Challenge Now: Ending the Missile Race
       (excerpts from message to the Congress on
       February 25, 1971)." US News and World Report 70
       (March 8, 1971): 53-54.

1394. "Towards Peace Through Arms Control (statement by the
       President, October 21, 1968)." War/Peace Report
       8 (December 1968): 10-13.

1395. "Treaty on the Nonproliferation of Nuclear Weapons
       Enters into Force (remarks on March 5, 1970)."
       Department of State Bulletin 62 (March 30, 1970):
       411-412.

1396. "Trip for World Peace (address on February 28,
       1972)." Vital Speeches 38 (March 15, 1972):
       322-323.

1397. "U.S. Balance of Payments (statement on April 14,
       1969)." Department of State Bulletin 60 (May 12,
       1969): 403-404.

1398. "United States Foreign Policy for the 1970s:
       Building for Peace (the president's address to
       the nation, February 25, 1971)." Weekly
       Compilation of Presidential Documents 7 (March 1,
       1971): 298-304.

1399. "U.S. Goals in International Trade and Monetary
       Affairs (excerpts from radio address on February
       21, 1973)." Department of State Bulletin 68
       (March 19, 1973): 321.

1400. "United States Oceans Policy (statement by the
       president, May 23, 1970)." Weekly Compilation of
       Presidential Documents 6 (May 25, 1970): 677-
       678.

1401. "United States--Peoples Republic of China (address on
       July 15, 1971)." Vital Speeches 37 (August 1,
       1971): 610.

1402. "United States Policy for the Seabed (statement on
       May 23, 1970)." Department of State Bulletin 62
       (June 15, 1970): 737-738.

1403. "U.S. Positions at Eighteen Nation Disarmament
       Conference (message on March 15, 1969)."
       Department of State Bulletin 60 (April 7, 1969):
       289-290.

158

1404. "Vietnam Plan (address on November 3, 1969)." Vital
       Speeches 36 (November 15, 1969): 66-70.

1405. "War in Vietnam (address on May 14, 1969)." Vital
       Speeches 35 (June 1, 1969): 482-484.

1406. "The War in Vietnam (the president's address to the
       nation, November 3, 1969)." Weekly Compilation
       of Presidential Documents 5 (November 10, 1969):
       1546-1555.

1407. "Wilsonian Principle After Half A Century (remarks on
       February 18, 1971)." Department of State
       Bulletin 64 (March 15, 1971): 312-314.

1408. "World and US Problems (address on July 6, 1971)."
       Vital Speeches 37 (August 1, 1971): 611-615.

Watergate

Watergate ended the presidency of Richard Milhous
Nixon. In 1972, Nixon was re-elected president of the
United States by the largest electoral margin ever achieved
up to that time. In 1974, Nixon was forced to resign the
presidency or face certain impeachment proceedings in the
U.S. Senate. Numerous works have appeared that detail the
facts of the Watergate scandal: Watergate: The Full Inside
Story (1974) by Lewis Chester et al.; Watergate: The
Waterloo of a President (1975) by Richard Hostrop; Breach of
Faith: the Fall of Richard Nixon (1975) by Theodore White.
Each of the major figures in the story have published their
particular version of the events. Richard Nixon published
RN, The Memoirs of Richard Nixon in 1978. Senator Sam
Ervin, who chaired the Senate Select Committee that
investigated the scandal, published his version The Whole
Truth: The Watergate Conspiracy in 1980. Judge John J.
Sirica, who broke the silence of the participants in the
actual break-in of the Watergate building, wrote To Set the
Record Straight: The Break-In, the Tapes, the Conspirator,
the Pardon in 1979. Leon Jaworski, the Special Prosecutor
for the Watergate legal investigation, wrote The Right and
the Power: The Prosecution of Watergate in 1976.

The number of books published relating to Watergate
both during the course of events and in subsequent years is
staggering. Kenyon and Judith Rosenberg's Watergate: An
Annotated Bibliography (1975) and Myron Smith, Jr.'s
Watergate: An Annotated Bibligraphy (1983) are excellent
compilations of both popular and scholarly works on the
Watergate scandal. Yet while numerous accounts of the
Watergate scandal have been published, there has been a
dearth of works that attempt to assess the meaning of
Watergate within the context of the American political and
social consciousness. Perhaps the assessment is not
possible until time has provided sufficient distance to
enable an objective analysis of the events and central
characters involved in the scandal, but theory and
interpretation are important missing elements, the absence
of which frustrates the researcher and leaves the average
reader with the choice only of antagonists of the Watergate
phenomenon, such as Leo Evans and Allen Myer's Watergate and
the Myth of American Democracy (1974) or Anthony Lukas's
Nightmare: The Dark Side of The Nixon Years (1976) or
William Vincent Shannon's They Could Not Trust the King:
Nixon, Watergate, and the American People (1974), for
interpretive analysis that centers on the personality of
Richard Nixon. Though Nixon's personality has been given
scholarly consideration as the key to interpreting the
Watergate scandal in such works as Frank Fox and Stephen

Parker's "Why Nixon Did Himself In: A Behavioral
Examination of His Need to Fail," which appeared in a
September 1974 issue of New York or Leo Pangell's article
for the Psychoanalytic Quarterly in 1976, "Lessons from
Watergate: A Derivative Psychoanalysis," the Nixon
personality alone does not account for the large number of
individuals and government agencies that were tainted by the
Watergate events.

There have been several attempts at placing the
Watergate scandal in the context of social theory. Among
these is the work of Jon Weiner. In his "Tocqueville, Marx,
Weber, and Nixon: Watergate in Theory," which appeared in
1976 issue of Dissent, Weiner assessed the significance of
Watergate for American politics and society by using the
framework supplied by several societal theorists.
Tocqueville's theory of the social contrast, Weiner argued,
would label Watergate as a violation of the rules for the
pluralistic politics of the American democratic system. In
this interpretation, Nixon lost the consensus of the
American public and the Republican Party through his actions
against political foes and thus fell from political power.
Weiner postulated that Marxist social theory would view
Watergate as a typical split in the ruling elites of
bourgeois society into two opposing factions differentiated
by economic interests. Weberian social theory, according to

Weiner, would view the Watergate scandal as a logical consequence in the growth of bureaucratic power. For Weber, Watergate would have been a conflict between the executive and legislative branches bureaucracies that ended with the legislative branch's reassertion of its rightful power.

Among the political theories advanced as the cause of the Watergate scandal is that contained in Michael Rogin's "The King's Two Bodies: Abraham Lincoln, Richard Nixon, and Presidential Self Sacrifice," which appeared in a 1979 issue of the Massachusetts Review. Rogin advances the interesting argument that Nixon merged the office of the presidency with his own person so that they seemed one and the same to him. Rogin contends that Nixon believed, as did Louis XIV, that he was the state. Due to public opinion concerns Nixon adopted Lincoln's Civil War position that "actions which would otherwise be unconstitutional, could become lawful if undertaken for the purpose of preserving the constitution and the nation." Though Rogin's article skillfully separates Nixon's actions from Lincoln's justification for his Civil War unconstitutional acts, the theory serves as a useful starting point for examination of weaknesses within the American political system that could lead to abuses of the social contract through adherence to past practice that cannot rationally be justified by present circumstances.

1409. Abramson, Harold J. "Watergate: Death at the Roots." Columbia Forum 3 (Winter 1974): 2-8.

1410. Arterton, F. Christopher. "Watergate and Children's Attitudes Toward Political Authority Revisited." Political Science Quarterly 90 (Fall 1975): 477-496.

1411. Axel-Lute, Paul. Checklist of Federal Documents on Watergate, Impeachment, and Presidential Transition, 1973-1974. Newark, NJ: P. Axel-Lute, 1975.

1412. Balfour, Nancy. "The U.S. Presidency in Danger." World Today 29 (December 1973): 505-513.

1413. Ball, Howard. No Pledge of Privacy: The Watergate Tapes Litigation. Port Washington, NY: Kennikat Press, 1972.

1414. Bates, J. Leonard. "Watergate and Teapot Dome." South Atlantic Quarterly 73 (Spring 1974): 145-159.

1415. Becker, Theodore L. "Watergate: On Campaigns and Government Anarchy." Society 10 (July 1973): 12-13.

1416. Benoit, William L. "Richard M. Nixon's Rhetorical Strategies in His Public Statements on Watergate." Southern Speech Communications Journal 47 (Winter 1982): 192-211.

1417. Bensman, Joseph. "Watergate: In the Corporate Style." Dissent 20 (Summer 1973): 279-280.

1418. Ben-Veniste, Richard, and George Frampton. Stonewall: The Inside Story of the Watergate Prosecution. New York, NY: Simon and Schuster, 1977.

1419. Bergman, Lowell, and Marwell Robach. "Nixon's Lucky City: C. Arnholdt Smith and the San Diego Connection." Ramparts Magazine 12 (October 1973): 32-35+.

1420. Bickel, Alexander M. "Watergate and the Legal Order." Commentary 57 (January 1974): 19-25.

1421. Bourjaily, Vance. "The Final Act." American Heritage. 35 (June/July 1984): 31-35.

1422. Boyan, A. Stephen. Constitutional Aspects of
       Watergate: Documents and Materials. Dobbs
       Ferry, NY: Oceana Publications, 1976.

1423. Boyd, Richard W., and David J. Hadler. "Presidential
       and Congressional Response to Political Crisis:
       Nixon, Congress, and Watergate." Congress and
       the Presidency 10 (Autumn 1983): 195-217.

1424. Branch, Taylor. "Crimes of Weakness." Harper's 248
       (October 1974): 40-43.

1425. _____. "Pleasure of Presidential Paraplegia."
       Harper 247 (September 1973): 57-58.

1426. Brower, Brock. "The Conscience of Leon Jaworski."
       Esquire 83 (February 1975): 89-97+.

1427. Brummet, Barry. "Presidential Substance: The
       Address of August 15, 1973." Western Speech 39
       (Fall 1975): 249-259.

1428. Brustern, Robert. "Greek Tragedy and the Watergate."
       New Republic 168 (May 26, 1973): 23.

1429. Bulman, Raymond F. "Love, Power, and the Justice of
       the U.S. Presidential Pardons." Journal of
       Church and State 21 (Winter 1979): 23-38.

1430. Burby, John F. "Conclusions Elusive as Initial Phase
       of Inquiry Ends." National Jouranl Reports 6
       (June 8, 1974): 857-860.

1431. _____. "Coverup Is Focus as Inquiry Nears Final
       Stage." National Journal Reports 6 (July 20,
       1974): 1065-1073.

1432. Buschel, Bruce, and William Vitka. Watergate File.
       New York, NY: Flash Books, 1973.

1433. Calhoon, Robert M. "Watergate and American
       Conservatism." South Atlantic Quarterly 83
       (Spring 1984): 127-137.

1434. Candee, Dan. "The Moral Psychology of Watergate."
       Journal of Social Issues 31 (Spring 1975): 183-
       192.

165

1435. Caraley, Demetrious, and Frances Penn. "Separation of Powers and Executive Privilege: The Watergate Briefs." Political Science Quarterly 88 (December 1973): 582-654.

1436. "Case for Resignation." Nation 216 (June 4, 1973): 706-707.

1437. Chester, Lewis, et al. Watergate: The Full Inside Story. New York, NY: Ballentine Books, 1974.

1438. Chomsky, Noam. "Watergate and Other Crimes." Ramparts Magazine 12 (June 1974): 31-36.

1439. Clancy, Paul R. Just a Country Lawyer: A Biography of Senator Sam Ervin. Bloomington, IN: Indiana University Press, 1974.

1440. Clark, Janet M. "Moral Prerequisites of Political Support: Business Reactions to the Watergate Scandal." Journal of Political Science 7, 1 (1979): 40-61.

1441. Clark, Leroy D. The Grand Jury: The Use and Abuse of Political Power. New York, NY: New York Times Book Company, 1975.

1442. Colson, Charles W. Born Again. New York, NY: Chosen Books, 1976.

1443. Dahlin, Robert. "Story Behind the Book, the Final Days." Publishers Weekly 209 (April 26, 1976): 42.

1444. Dean, John. Blind Ambition. New York, NY: Simon and Schuster, 1976.

1445. Dewsnap, Terrence. "Watergate Endings and Initiations." Biography 6 (Fall 1983): 342-352.

1446. Diamond, Edwin. "Tape Shock: The Nixon Transcripts." Columbia Journalism Review 13 (July/August 1974): 5-9.

1447. Dougherty, John E. "Nixon's Ultimate Option: Possibility of a Military Coup." Progressive 38 (February 1974): 7-8.

1448. Drew, Elizabeth. Washington Journal: The Events 1973-1974. New York, NY: Random House, 1975.

1449. Drossman, Evan, et al. Watergate and the White House: July-December 1973 vol. II. New York, NY: Facts on File, 1974.

1450. Ervin, Sam J. The Whole Truth: The Watergate Conspiracy. New York, NY: Random House, 1980.

1451. Evans, Les. "Watergate and the White House: From Kennedy to Nixon and Beyond." International Socialist Review 34 (December 1973): 4-11; 25-40.

1452. Evans, Les, and Allen Myers. Watergate and the Myth of American Democracy. New York, NY: Pathfinder Press, 1974.

1453. Failie, Henry. "Lessons of Watergate: On the Possibility of Morality in Politics." Encounter 43 (October 1974): 8027.

1454. Fox, Frank, and Stephen Parker. "Why Nixon Did Himself In: A Behavioral Examination of His Need to Fail." New York 6 (September 9, 1974): 26-32.

1455. Friedman, Leon. United States vs Nixon: The President Before the Supreme Court. New York, NY: Bowker, 1974.

1456. Gouran, Dennis, S. "The Watergate Cover-up: Its Dynamics and Its Implications." Communication Monographs 43 (August 1976): 176-186.

1457. "Government of Laws or Men? Decisions to Hand over Watergate Tapes." America 129 (November 3, 1973): 319.

1458. Haldeman, Harry R. Ends of Power. Boston, MA: G.K. Hall, 1978.

1459. Halpern, Paul J. Why Watergate? Pacific Palisades, CA: Palisades Publishers, 1975.

1460. Harrell, Jackson, B.L. Ware, and Wil A. Linkugel. "Failure of Apology in American Politics: Nixon Watergate." Speech Monographs 42 (November 1975): 245-261.

1461. Harrington, Michael. "Watergate: On Politics and Money." Dissent 20 (Summer 1973): 278-279.

1462. Harward, Donald W. Crisis in Confidence: The Impact of Watergate. Boston, MA: Little, Brown and Company, 1974.

1463. "Has President Nixon Extended Doctrine of Executive Privilege Too Far?" Congressional Quarterly Weekly Reports 31 (April 14, 1973): 864-865.

1464. Hawkins, Robert P., Suzanne Piagree, and Donald F. Robert. Watergate and Political Stabilization: The Inescapable Event." American Politics Quarterly 3 (October 1975): 406-422.

1465. Hershey, Majorie Randon, and David B. Hall. "Watergate and Pre-Adults' Attitudes Toward the President." American Journal of Political Science 19 (November 1975): 703-726.

1466. Higgins, George V. "The Friends of Richard Nixon and How He Conned Them." Atlantic 234 (November 1974): 41-52.

1467. _____. The Friends of Richard Nixon. Boston, MA: Little, Brown and Company, 1975.

1468. Hillman, Ben. "Nixon Wields the Hatchet." Dissent 20 (Spring 1973): 132-136.

1469. Hostrop, Richard W. Watergate: The Waterloo of a President. Palm Springs, CA: ETC Publications, 1975.

1470. Hunt, E. Howard. Undercover: Memoirs of an American Secret Agent. New York, NY: GP Putnam's Sons, 1974.

1471. Hurwitz, Leon, Barbara Green, and Hans. E. Segal. "International Press Reactions to the Resignation and Pardon of Richard M. Nixon: A Content Analysis of Four Elite Newspapers." Comparative Politics 9 (October 1976): 107-123.

1472. Jaworski, Leon. The Right and the Power: The Presecution of Watergate. New York, NY: Reader's Digest Press, 1976.

1473. Johnson, Gerald W. "Watergate: One End, But Which?" American Scholar 42 (Autumn 1973): 594-603.

1474. Kammerman, Roy. Poor Richard's Watergate. Los Angeles, CA: Price/Stern/Sloan, 1973.

1475. Katula, Richard A. "Apology of Richard M. Nixon."
       Today's Speech 23 (Fall 1975): 1-5.

1476. Kazee, Thomas A. "Television Exposure and Attitude
       Change: The Impact of Political Interest."
       Public Opinion Quarterly 45 (Winter 1981): 507-
       518.

1477. Kelly, Alfred. "History as Teacher." American
       History 4, 1 (1976): 132-137.

1478. Klump, James F., and Jeffrey F. Lukehart. "The
       Pardoning of Richard Nixon: A Failure in
       Motivational Strategy." Western Journal of
       Speech and Communication 42 (Spring 1978): 116-
       123.

1479. Knappman, Edward W. Watergate and the White House, 3
       vols. New York, NY: Facts on File, 1975.

1480. Kolodney, David. "Gerald Ford, Under Study for
       Defeat." Ramparts Magazine 13 (October 1974):
       8-13.

1481. Kwong, Chan-Ying, and Kenneth Starch. "New York
       Times' Stance on Nixon and Public Opinion."
       Journalism Quarterly 53 (Winter 1976): 723-727.

1482. Lang, Gladys E., and Kurt Lang. The Battle for
       Public Opinion: The President, the Press, and
       the Polls During Watergate. New York, NY:
       Columbia University Press, 1983.

1483. _____. "Polling on Watergate: The Battle for
       Public Opinion." Public Opinion Quarterly 44
       (Winter 1980): 530-547.

1484. Lardner, George. "Behind the Scenes at the Cox
       Investigation." Ramparts Magazine 12 (January
       1974): 21-26.

1485. Lewin, Nathan. "Subpoenaing the President." New
       Republic 168 (June 9, 1973): 19-21.

1486. Lieberman, Myron. "Watergate: The Bottom Line."
       Alternative 8 (December 1974): 18-20.

1487. Lipset, Seymour, and Earl Raab. "An Appointment with
       Watergate." Commentary 56 (September 1973): 35-
       43.

1488. Lukas, J. Anthony. Nightmare: the Dark Side of the
       Nixon Years, 1969-1974. New York, NY: Viking
       Press, 1976.

1489. Lynch, Mitchell, and Albert Hunt. "The End: Ford
       Pardons Nixon, Move on Watergate Jolts His
       Honeymoon." Wall Street Journal 184 (September
       9, 1974): 1+.

1490. McCarthy, Mary. Mask of State: Watergate Protraits.
       New York, NY: Harcourt Brace Jovanovich, 1974.

1491. McCord, James W. Piece of Tape: The Watergate
       Story: Fact and Fiction. Washington, DC:
       Washington Media Services, 1974.

1492. Magnuson, Edward. "Post-mortem: The Unmaking of a
       President." Time 105 (May 12, 1975): 72+.

1493. Magruder, Jeb. An American Life: One Man's Road to
       Watergate. New York, NY: Barnes and Noble,
       1974.

1494. Mankiewicz, Frank. The Final Crisis of Richard M.
       Nixon. New York, NY: Quadrangle Book, 1974.

1495. _____. U.S. vs. Richard M. Nixon: The Final
       Crisis. New York, NY: Quadrangle, 1975.

1496. Mankoff, Milton. "Watergate and Sociological
       Theory." Theory and Society 1 (Spring 1974):
       103-109.

1497. "Many Questions Remain: Failure of Operation
       Candor." Nation 217 (December 10, 1973): 610-
       612.

1498. May, John D. "The Congressional Watergate Case."
       Australian Quarterly 46, 1 (March 1974): 54-58.

1499. Mayer, Milton. "An American Banality." Center
       Magazine 8 (May 1975): 2-5.

1500. Miller, Arthur S. "Limited Hang Out: The Dialogues
       of Richard Nixon as a Drama of the Anti-Hero."
       Harper's 249 (September 1974): 13-14+.

1501. Miller, Ben R. "The Presidency and Separation of
       Powers." American Bar Association Journal 60
       (February 1974): 195-197.

1502. Miller, Marvin. The Breaking of a President, 5 vols.
       City of Industry, CA: Therapy Productions, 1974.

1503. Miller, William L. "Some Notes on Watergate and
       America." Yale Review 63 (Spring 1974): 321-
       322.

1504. "Mr. Nixon Resigns." America 131 (August 24, 1974):
       62-63.

1505. Moellering, R.L. "Civil Religion, the Nixon
       Theology and the Watergate Scandal." Christian
       Century 90 (September 26, 1973): 947-948+.

1506. Mollenhoff, Clark R. Game Plan for Disaster: An
       Ombudsman's Report on the Nixon Years. New York,
       NY: Norton, 1976.

1507. Monaghan, Frank. Poor Richard's Paradox. New York,
       NY: Alpha Publishing Company, 1974.

1508. Myerson, Michael. Watergate: Crime in the Suites.
       New York, NY: International Publications, 1973.

1509. Neal, Fred W. "The Cold War: Road to Watergate."
       Center Magazine 6 (September 1973): 19-23.

1510. The New York Times. End of a Presidency. New York,
       NY: Holt Rinehart, Winston, 1974.

1511. The New York Times. The Watergate Hearings: Break-
       in and Cover-up. New York, NY: Viking Press,
       1973.

1512. Nikolaieff, George A. The President and the
       Constitution. New York, NY: H.W. Wilson, 1974.

1513. "Nixon on Watergate." Time 106 (July 7, 1975): 10.

1514. "Nixon's Role in Watergate." US News and World
       Report 75 (July 9, 1973): 11-13.

1515. "Non-government and Resignation." Commonweal 99
       (January 18, 1973): 370-380.

1516. O'Brien, Robert W., and Elizabeth J. Jones. Night
       Nixon Spoke: a Study of Political Effectiveness.
       Los Alamitos, Ca: Hwong Publishers, 1977.

1517. "On the Merits: Possibility of Prosecuting R.M.
      Nixon." Nation 219 (September 14, 1974): 194-
      195.

1518. Osborne, John. "Back to Work: Restoring Confidence
      in the President." New Republic 169 (September
      22, 1973): 13-15.

1519. _____. "Pardon." New Republic 171 (September 28,
      1974): 9-11.

1520. _____. "Searing Wound: Forced Resignation of
      J.D. Erlichman and H.R. Haldeman." New Republic
      168 (May 26, 1973): 15-17.

1521. Overland, Doris. "Great Watergate Conspiracy! A TV
      Blitzkrieg?" Contemporary Review 233 (July
      1978): 29-32.

1522. Paletz, David. "Television Drama: The Appeals of
      the Senate Watergate Hearings." Midwest
      Quarterly 21 (Autumn 1979): 63-70.

1523. Pangell, Leo. "Lessons from Watergate. A Derivative
      Psychoanalysis." Pschoanalytic Quarterly 45
      (January 1976): 37-61.

1524. "A Pardon for Nixon and Watergate Is Back."
      Congressional Quarterly Weekly Reports 32
      (September 14, 1974): 2454-2463.

1525. "People of the United States of America v. Richard
      Milhous Nixon." Progressive 38 (January 1974):
      5-7.

1526. Peters, Charles. "Blind Ambition at the White
      House." Washington Monthly 9 (March 1977): 17-
      21.

1527. Pincus, Walter. "Drippings from the Watergate." New
      Republic 169 (July 28, 1973): 10-13,

1528. "Political Strategy." Nation 217 (December 3, 1973):
      578-580.

1529. Rangell, Leo. The Mind of Watergate: An Exploration
      of the Compromise of Integrity. New York, NY:
      W.W. Norton, 1980.

1530. "Reflections on the Resignation: A Symposium."
      National Review 26 (August 30, 1974): 954-962+.

1531. "Reselling the President." Time 102 (July 9, 1973):
       20-21.

1532. Richardson, Elliot. "The Saturday Nigh Massacre."
       Atlantic 237 (March 1976): 40-41+.

1533. Riemer, Neal. "Watergate and Prophetic Politics."
       Review of Politics 36 (April 1974): 284-297.

1534. Rogin, Michael P. "The King's Two Bodies: Abraham
       Lincoln, Richard Nixon, and Presidential Self-
       Sacrifice." Massachusetts Review 20 (Autumn
       1979): 553-573.

1535. Rosenbaum, Ron. "Ah, Watergate." New Republic 187
       (June 1982): 15-24.

1536. Rosenberg, Harold. "Thugs Adrift." Partisan Review
       40, 3 (1973): 341-348.

1537. Rosenberg, Kenyon C., and Judith K. Rosenberg.
       Watergate: An Annotated Bibliography.
       Littleton, CO: Libraries Unlimited, 1975.

1538. Rosenberg, Leonard B. "Luck or Design: The Fall of
       Richard M. Nixon." Politics 40, 4 (1975): 706-
       709.

1539. "Round 2 in Nixon's Counterattack." Time 102
       (December 3, 1973): 14-17.

1540. Royster, Vermont. "Public Morality: After Thoughts
       on Watergate." Southern Exposure 1 (Summer/Fall
       1973): 2-8.

1541. Sale, Kirkpatrick. "The Sunshine Syndicate Behind
       Watergate." Southern Exposure 1 (Summer/Fall
       1973): 2-8.

1542. Schapper, Morris B. Conscience of the Nation: The
       People Versus Richard M. Nixon. Washington, DC:
       Public Affairs Press, 1974.

1543. Shannon, William Vincent. They Could Not Trust the
       King: Nixon, Watergate, and the American
       People. New York, NY: Collier Books, 1974.

1544. Shawcross, William. "Tyrant in the White House."
       New Statesman 85 (January 19, 1973): 75-76.

1545. _____. "Will Checkers Ride Again?" New Statesman and Nation 85 (April 27, 1973): 603-604.

1546. Sheehan, John F. "Ammesty of President Nixon?" America 129 (August 4, 1973): 67-68.

1547. Sherrill, Robert G. "Zealots for Nixon: Gaudy Night at the Watergate." Nation 215 (September 25, 1972): 230-234.

1548. Shirer, William L. "Hubris of a President." Nation 216 (January 22, 1973): 105-108.

1549. Sirica, John J. To Set the Record Straight: the Break-in, the Tapes, the Conspirator, the Pardon. New York, NY: Norton, 1979.

1550. Smith, Myron, Jr. Watergate: An Annotated Bibliography. Metuchen, NJ: Scarecrow Press, 1983.

1551. Stein, Howard A. "The Silent Complicity at Watergate." American Scholar 43 (Winter 1973): 21-37.

1552. Stephenson, David. "The Mild Magistracy of the Law: U.S. versus Richard Nixon." International Problems 103 (February 1975): 288-292.

1553. Stoval, James G. "Conflict in the Colonies: The London Times Coverage of Watergate from the Break-in to the Pardon." Gazette 25, 4 (1979): 209-218.

1554. Sussman, Barry. The Great Cover-up: Nixon and the Scandal of Watergate. New York, NY: New American Library, 1974.

1555. Thompson, Fred. At That Point in Time: The Inside Story of the Watergate Committee. New York, NY: Quadrangle Books, 1975.

1556. Todd, William B. "The White House Transcripts." Papers of the Bibliographic Society of America 68, 3 (1974): 268-296.

1557. "The Triumph of Watergate." American Heritage. 35 (June/July 1984): 22-35.

1558. Tucker, John Robert. Bicentennial Tragedy: An
          Indictment of the Law. Hicksville, NY:
          Exportion Press, 1977.

1559. Ungar, Sanford J. "Undoing of the Justice
          Department." Atlantic 233 (January 1974): 29-
          34.

1560. "Unpardonable." Progressive 38 (October 1974): 5-6.

1561. "Unpardonable Offenses." New Republic 171 (September
          21, 1974): 5-6.

1562. Van Alstyne, William. "President Nixon: Toughing it
          out with the Law." American Bar Association
          Journal 59 (December 1973): 1398-1402.

1563. Viorst, Milton. "Tapes, Tricks, and Spiro: Oval
          Room Machiavelli." Nation 217 (October 22,
          1973): 398-401.

1564. The Washington Post. The Fall of a President. New
          York, NY: Delacorte Press, 1974.

1565. "Watergate: An End of an Epoch." Current 155
          (October 1973): 16-20.

1566. "The Watergate Experience: Lessons for Empirical
          Theory." American Politics Quarterly 3 (October
          1975): 355-476.

1567. Watergate, Politics, and the Legal Process.
          Washington, DC: American Enterprise Institute
          for Public Policy Research, 1974.

1568. "Watergate Prosecutors Tell Why Nixon Was Not
          Indicted." US News and World Report 79 (October
          27, 1975): 65-66.

1569. Watergate: The View from the Left. New York, NY:
          Pathfinder, 1973.

1570. Western, Alan, and John Shattuck. "The Second
          Deposing of Richard Nixon." Civil Liberties
          Review 3 (June/July 1976: 8-23; 84-96.

1571. White, Theodore H. Breach of Faith: The Fall of
          Richard Nixon. New York, NY: Atheneum, 1975.

1572.   "White House Death Watch: Press Coverage of Nixon's
        Resignation." Newsweek 84 (August 19, 1974):
        77-78

1573.   Wiener, Jon. "Tocqueville, Marx, Weber, Nixon:
        Watergate in Theory." Dissent 23 (Spring 1976):
        171-180.

1574.   Wilson, Gerald L. "The Strategy of Explanation:
        Richard M. Nixon's August 8, 1974 Resignation
        Speech." Communications Quarterly 24 (Summer
        1976): 14-20.

1575.   Winter, Ruth. "Scientists Analyze The Voices of
        Nixon, Haldeman, Ehrlichman, And Dean." Science
        Digest 89 (June 1976): 62-68.

1576.   Woodward, C. Vann. Responses of the Presidents to
        Charges of Misconduct: White House Under Fire.
        New York, NY: Delacorte Press, 1974.

1577.   Woodward, Bob, and Carl Bernstein. The Final Days.
        New York, NY: Simon and Schuster, 1976.

1578.   "A World Without Nixon." Economist 252 (August 3,
        1974): 11-12.

1579.   Wright, Esmond. "The United States after Watergate."
        Contemporary Review 225 (November 1974): 231-
        237.

1580.   Zimmer, Troy A. "The Impact of Watergate on the
        Public's Trust in People and Confidence in the
        Mass Media." Social Science Quarterly 59 (March
        1979): 743-751.

Speeches - Watergate

1581.   "Address to the American People (the president's
        resignation speech, August 8, 1974)." Weekly
        Compilation of Presidential Documents 10 (August
        12, 1974): 1014-1017.

1582.   "I Accept the Court's Decision (statement on Supreme
        Court decision concerning tapes on July 24,
        1974)." US News and World Report 77 (August 5,
        1974): 17.

1583. "Nixon's Address to Nation on the Watergate Case
       (radio and television address on August 15,
       1973)." Vital Speeches 39 (September 1, 1973):
       674-677.

1584. "Nixon's Farewell (address on August 8, 1974)." Vital
       Speeches 40 (August 15, 1974): 643-644.

1585. "Presidential Tapes and Documents (statement by the
       president, November 12, 1973)." Weekly
       Compilation of Presidential Document 9 (November
       19, 1973): 1329-1331.

1586. "Presidential Tapes and Materials (address on April
       29, 1974)." Vital Speeches 40 (June 1, 1974):
       482-486.

1587. "Regret, Pain, Anguish (statement after being
       pardoned by President Ford on September 8,
       1974)." Newsweek 84 (September 16, 1974): 20-
       21.

1588. "Subpoena of Presidential Tapes and Materials (the
       president's address to the nation, April 29,
       1974)." Weekly Compilation of Presidential
       Documents 10 (May 6, 1974): 450-458.

1589. "Watergate Affair (radio and television address on
       April 30, 1973)." Vital Speeches 39 (May 15,
       1973): 450-452.

1590. "The Watergate Investigation (statement by the
       President, August 15, 1973)." Weekly Compilation
       of Presidential Documents 9 (August 20, 1973):
       991-994.

Impeachment

Impeachment proceedings against Richard Nixon began in
the summer of 1974. There are several accounts of the
events that brought Nixon from an unnamed co-conspirator in
the Watergate complex break-in to the point of being
impeached by the House of Representatives for high crimes
and misdemeanors as president. Jimmy Breslin wrote How the
Good Guys Finally Won: Notes from an Impeachment Summer in
1976. The Final Days by Bernstein and Woodward also
appeared in 1976. Prior to the actual impeachment
proceedings conducted by the House, several works attempted
to define and set procedures for an impeachment of a
president. Edwin Firmage wrote "The Law of Presidential
Impeachment" for the Utah Law Review in 1973. Also in 1973,
Albert Broderick wrote "Citizen's Guide to the Impeachment
of the President" for the Catholic University Law Review.
Charles Black published in early 1974 Impeachment: A
Handbook. Many political analysts were urging an
impeachment of Richard Nixon from the early spring of 1974.
Harper's published an article by Taylor Branch, "Why We Will
Impeach Him," in May of 1974. Robert Leggett wrote an
article for the May 1974 issue of the Progressive entitled
"Nixon's Case Against Nixon: The President's Own Admission
Provides Enough Evidence to Impeach Him." In June of 1974,

Henry Commager's "Five Grounds for Impeaching the President"
was read into the Congressional Record. While other noted
political observers of the crisis were urging a resignation
in opposition to the impeachment remedy. William F. Buckley
argued in a 1973 issue of the New York Times Magazine
"Impeach the Speech, Not the President." Nation argued "The
Case for Resignation," as early as June of 1973. Time also
speculated "Impeach or Resign: Voices in a Historic
Controversy," in 1973.

During the 1974 impeachment crisis, political analysts
were convinced of Nixon's guilt. A survey of public opinion
in the fall of 1973 confirmed that the nation as a whole was
also convinced of the President's involvement on the
Watergate break-in and cover-up. These findings were
published by Patrick McGeever and Gerald Ford in their
article "Guilty Yes: Impeachment No: Some Empirical
Findings," for Political Science Quarterly in June of 1974.
McGeever's article revealed that two-thirds of those
surveyed believed that Nixon was guilty but that only one-
third of those surveyed wanted Nixon removed from office
through impeachment or resignation. Even more startling for
McGeever was the fact that forty percent of those surveyed
would vote for Nixon and only twenty-five percent would vote
for McGovern, Nixon's 1972 campaign opponent if the
presidential election were being held at the time of the
survey, September of 1973.

Nixon's resignation of the presidency in August of 1974
ended the impeachment crisis. The full House of
Representatives never voted on the articles of impeachment
passed by the Impeachment Committee but merely voted to
accept the committee's report. This fact was protested by
many Nixon critics at the time. Gardner Cromwell had a
memorandum placed in the Congressional Record in September
of 1974 entitled "Constitutional Responsibility of Congress
to Pursue Impeachment and Trial Remedies in a Proceeding
Once Commenced or After a President Resigns." Representing
John Conyers wrote an article for the Black Scholar in 1974
explaining "Why Nixon Should Have Been Impeached."

1591. Alpern, David M., and Richard M. Smith. "All About
        Impeachment." Newsweek 83 (March 25, 1974): 28-
        35.

1592. Alsop, Stewart. "I Would Not Want the Presidency on
        Those Terms." Newsweek 83 (May 21, 1973): 108.

1593. American Civil Liberties Union. Why Nixon Should Be
        Impeached. Washington, DC: Public Affairs
        Press, 1973.

1594. "Articles of Impeachment." Congressional Record 120
        (August 22, 1974): H8967-8968.

1595. Berger, Raoul. "Impeachment: An Instrument of
        Regeneration--How It Works and Why It Must Be
        Used Now." Harper's 2 48 (January 1974): 14, 16,
        18-19, 22.

1596. _____. Impeachment: The Constitutional Problems.
        New York, NY: Bantam 1974.

1597. Black, Charles L. Impeachment: A Handbook. New
        Haven, CT: Yale University Press, 1974.

1958. Bonafede, Dom. "Anti-Impeachment Plans Focus on Law, Politics, and Media." National Journal Reports 6 (May 11, 1974): 685-691.

1599. Branch, Taylor. "Why We Will Impeach Him." Harper 248 (May 1974): 23-24+

1600. Breslin, Jimmy. How the Good Guys Finally Won: Notes from an Impeachment Summer. New York, NY: Ballantine Books, 1976.

1601. Broderick, Albert. "Citizen's Guide to the Impeachment of the President." Catholic University Law Review 23 (Winter 1973): 205-254.

1602. _____. "the Politics of Impeachment." American Bar Association Journal 60 (May 1974): 554-556+.

1603. _____. "What Are Impeachable Offenses?" American Bar Association Journal 60 (April 1974): 415-419.

1604. Buckley, William F. "Impeach the Speech, Not the President." New York Times Magazine (May 20, 1973): 30+.

1605. Burby, John F., and Richard E. Cohen. "Three Articles Voted by Judiciary Committee." National Journal Reports 6 (August 3, 1974): 1141-1154.

1606. "Case for Resignation." Nation 216 (June 4, 1973): 706-707.

1607. Commager, Henry Steel. "Five Grounds for Impeaching the President: An Address." Congressional Record 120 (June 28, 1974): 21767-21768.

1608. Conyers, John. "Views on Impeachment." Freedomways 14, 4 (1974): 303-313.

1609. _____. "Why Nixon Should Have Been Impeached." Black Scholar 6 (October 1974): 2-8.

1610. Costello, Mary. "Presidential Impeachment." Editorial Research Reports (December 5, 1973): 925-946.

1611. Cromwell, Gardner. "Constitutional Responsibilities of Congress to Pursue Impeachment and Trial Remedies in a Proceeding Once Commenced or After a President Resigns: Memorandum." Congressional Record 120 (September 17, 1974): 31346-31348.

1612. Danielson, George E. "Presidential Immunity from Criminal Prosecution." Georgetown Law Journal 63 (May 1975): 1065-1069.

1613. Diamond, Robert A. Impeachment and the US Congress. Washington, DC: Congressional Quarterly, Inc., 1974

1614. Dobrovir, William A., et al. The Offenses of Richard M. Nixon: A Lawyer's Guide for the People of the United States of America. Washington, DC: A.B. Zill, 1973.

1615. "Everything You Wanted to Know About Impeachment but Were Afraid To Ask." Time 102 (November 5, 1973): 32-33.

1616. "Evidence: Fitting the Pieces Together." Time 104 (July 22, 1974): 20-25.

1617. Falk, Richard A. "Why Impeachment?" New Republic 165 (May 1, 1971): 13-14.

1618. Firmage, Edwin Brown. "The Law of Presidential Impeachment." Utah Law Review 24 (Winter 1973): 681-704.

1619. Flatto, Elie. "Impeachment of a President: Reflections on Watergate." Contemporary Review 223 (September 1973): 129-131.

1620. _____. "Impeachment of Richard M. Nixon." Contemporary Review 226 (March 1975): 146-148.

1621. Fry, Brian R., and John S. Stolarek. "The Impeachment Process: Predispositions and Votes." Journal of Politics 42 (November 1980): 1118-1134.

1622. _____. "The Nixon Impeachment Vote: A Speculative Analysis." Presidential Studies Quarterly 11 (Summer 1981): 387-394.

1623. Granberg, Donald. "An Analysis of the House
       Judiciary Committee's Recommendation to Impeach
       Richard Nixon." Political Psychology 2
       (Fall/Winter 1980): 50-65.

1624. Griffith, Thomas. "Proper Grounds for Impeachment."
       Time 103 (February 25, 1974): 23-24.

1625. "Grounds for Impeachment?" Newsweek 82 (November 5,
       1973): 32+.

1626. "House Study Sets Broad Grounds for Impeachment." US
       News and World Report 66 (March 4, 1974): 25-26.

1627. "If Nixon Is Impeached, What Then?" US News and
       World Report 76 (February 4, 1974): 22-29.

1628. "Impeach Nixon: Three Views in a Historic Debate."
       US News and World Report 76 (February 25, 1974):
       20-22.

1629. "Impeach or Resign: Voices in a Historic
       Controversy." Time 102 (November 19, 1973): 20-
       21.

1630. "Impeachment--A Trial for the Nation." Reader's
       Digest 105 (September 1974): 61-63.

1631. "Impeachment and the House." New Republic 169
       (November 3, 1973): 5-7.

1632. "Impeachment: Congress Puts Nixon Under a
       Microscope." US News and World Report 76
       (February 18, 1974): 27-29.

1633. "Impeachment Crisis--A Historic Debate Before the
       Supreme Court." US News and World Report 77
       (July 22, 1974): 72-75.

1634. "Impeachment Crisis--Key Decisions at Hand." US News
       and World Report 77 (July 22, 1974): 15-17.

1635. "Impeachment: Down to the Real Issues." US News and
       World Report 77 (July 29, 1974): 16-18.

1636. "Impeachment Fight--The President Comes Out
       Swinging." US News and World Report 76 (January
       21, 1974): 16-17.

1637. "Impeachment Focus." National Review 26 (July 19,
       1974): 793-794.

1638. "Impeachment Lobby: Emphasis on Grass Roots
          Pressure." Congressional Quarterly Weekly Report
          32 (May 25, 1974): 1368-1380.

1639. "Impeachment: Men on the Spot." Newsweek 84 (July
          15, 1974): 14-18+.

1640. "Impeachment: Moving Toward a Decision."
          Congressional Quarterly Weekly Report 3 (July 27,
          1974): 1923-1946.

1641. "The Impeachment of Richard Nixon." New Republic 170
          (March 16, 1974): 5-8.

1642. "Impeachment: Phase One." Newsweek 83 (May 20,
          1974): 28+.

1643. "Impeachment: The Case Unfolds." Newsweek 83 (May
          27, 1974): 26+.

1644. "Impeachment: Three Articles Sent to the House
          Floor." Congressional Quarterly Weekly Report 32
          (August 3, 1974): 2007-2023.

1645. Joesten, Joachim. The Assorted Crimes of Richard M.
          Nixon. West Germany: Haus, 1973.

1646. Jones, Stephen. "Was Richard Nixon Guilty? The Case
          for the Defense." Oklahoma Bar Association
          Journal 49 (Winter 1978): 251-268.

1647. Johnston, Gerald W. "Impeachment?" New Republic
          164 (April 10, 1971): 14-15.

1648. Kurland, Philip B. "Watergate Impeachment and the
          Constitution." Mississippi Law Review 45 (May
          1974): 531+.

1649. Labovitz, John R. Presidential Impeachment. New
          Haven CT: Yale University Press, 1978.

1650. Laing, Robert B., and Robert L. Stevenson. "Public
          Opinion Trends in the Last Days of the Nixon
          Administration: Those Who Viewed Hearings Were
          More Likely to Favor Impeachment and More Likely
          to Base Opinion on Information About Watergate."
          Journalism Quarterly 53 (Summer 1976): 294-302.

1651. Lawler, John. "Watergate: The Eighteenth Brumaire
       of Richard Nixon." Political Affairs 53
       (February 1974): 34-45.

1652. Leggett, Robert L. "Nixon's Case Against Nixon: The
       President's Own Admission Provides Enough Evidence
       To Impeach Him." Progressive 38 (May 1974): 15-
       18.

1653. "Let's Not Impeach the Nixon Mandate." Fortune 89
       (June 1974): 119-120.

1654. Lewin, Miriama, and Maura Kane. "Impeachment of
       Nixon and the Risky Shift." International
           Journal of Group Tensions 5 (September 1975):
       171-176.

1655. Laurie, Leonard. The Impeachment of Richard Nixon.
       New York, NY: Berkley Publishing Corporation,
       1973.

1656. McGeever, Patrick J., and Gerald B. Finch. "Guilty
       Yes: Impeachment No." Political Science
       Quarterly 89 (June 1974): 289-304.

1657. McWhinney, Edward. "Congress and the Presidency and
       the Impeachment Power." Indiana Law Review 8
       (1974): 833-851.

1658. McWilliams, Carey. "Real Richard: Tapes as an Air
       Tight Case for Impeachment." Nation 218 (May 18,
       1974): 610-612.

1659. Mezvinsky, Edward M., and Doris S. Freedman.
       "Federal Income Tax Invasion as an Impeachable
       Offence." Georgetown Law Journal 63, 5 (May
       1975): 1071-1081.

1660. Miller, Arthur S. "The Coming Trial of Richard M.
       Nixon." Progressive 38 (June 1974): 15-18.

1661. Neal, Fred W. "A Liberal's Case for Keeping the
       President." Center Magazine 7 (May 1974): 4-11.

1662. _____. "Keeping Nixon for Detente's Sake."
       Current 159 (February 1974): 11-16.

1663. "Politics, Morality and Impeachment." America 130
       (March 16, 1974): 182-183.

1664. Rhodes, Irwin S. "What Really Happened to the
       Jefferson Subpoenas?" American Bar Association
       Journal 60 (January 1974): 52-54.

1665. St. Clair, James, et al. An Analysis of the
       Constitutional Standard for Presidential
       Impeachment. Washington, DC: Government
       Printing Office, 1974.

1666. Saxbe, William. "If Nixon Is Impeached--What Then?"
       US News and World Report 76 (February 4, 1974):
       22-26+.

1667. Schlesinger, Arthur. "What If We Don't Impeach Him?"
       Harper 248 (May 1974): 12-18.

1668. Schnapper, Morris. Conscience of the Nation: The
       People Versus Richard M. Nixon. Washington, DC:
       Public Affairs Press, 1974.

1669. _____. Presidential Impeachment: A Documentary
       Overview. Washington, DC: Public Affairs Press,
       1974.

1670. "The Senate Prepares to Judge." Time 104 (August 12,
       1974): 12.

1671. Shapiro, Walter. "The Ziegler Memorandum: Five
       Point Plan to Prevent Impeachment." Washington
       Monthly 5 (January 1974): 40-46.

1672. Stern, Laurence. "Why Nixon Must Fall." New
       Statesman 88 (August 2, 1974): 139-140.

1673. Stone, Isidor F. "Impeachment." New York Review of
       Books (June 28, 1973): 12-19.

1674. Strackbein, Oscar Robert. "Crime as the Sole Basis
       of Impeachment." Congressional Record 120 (April
       3, 1974): 9694-9695.

1675. _____. "Impeachment--A Primitive Political
       Weapon." Congressional Record 120 (April 24,
       1974): 11795-11796.

1676. _____. "Impeachment as a Political Weapon."
       Congressional Record 120 (April 24, 1974):
       11795-11796.

186

1677. _____. "Impeachment Perspective--Looking in the
      Mirror of History ." Congressional Record 120
      (May 23, 1974): 16285.

1678. _____. "Why Impeachment?" Congressional Record
      120 (July 17, 1974): 2888-28889.

1679. Stringfellow, William. "Impeach Nixon Now."
      Commonweal 96 (May 26, 1972): 280-281.

1680. Tuchman, Barbara W. "Need for Impeachment?" Current
      155 (October 1973): 26-28.

1681. US Congress--House--Committee on the Judiciary.
      Brief on Behalf of the President of the United
      States. Washington, DC: US Government Printing
      Office, 1974.

1682. _____. Debate on the Articles of
      Impeachment. Washington, DC: US Government
      Printing Office, 1974.

1683. _____. Impeachment of Richard M. Nixon
      President of the United States: Report of the
      Committee on the Judiciary. Washington, DC: US
      Government Printing Office, 1974.

1684. _____. Minority Memorandum on Facts and
      Law. Washington, D.C.: US Government Printing
      Office, 1974.

1685. Van Alstyne, William. "The Third Impeachment
      Article: Congressional Boots Trapping."
      American Bar Association Journal 60 (October
      1974): 1199-1202.

1686. Wainer, Howard. "Predicting the Outcome of the
      Senate Trial of Richard M. Nixon." Behavioral
      Science 19 (November 1974): 404-406.

1687. Wright, George C. "Constituency Response to
      Congressional Behaivor: The Impact of the House
      Judiciary Committee Impeachment Votes." Western
      Political Quarterly 30 (September 1977): 401-
      410.

Revisionist History

In May of 1987, Richard Nixon was inducted into the
Académie des Beaux Arts of France for his assistance when
president of the United States in securing funds to restore
French historic monuments. A span of a mere thirteen years
saw Nixon rise from the ignominy of resigning the presidency
of the United States due to scandal and alleged illegal
activities to receiving the highest honor that French
culture could bestow. Though such reversal of fortune is
common in Nixon's life, it certainly was not foreseeable in
1974 that public respect and even admiration for Nixon's
presidency would resurface during his lifetime. It cannot
be denied that Richard Nixon has aggressively set out to
redeem his place in history. Numerous books, interviews,
and foreign trips by the former president have all had the
goal of reversing public opinion about the Nixon image, but
that within so short a period of time, others--political
analysts, historians, and public agencies--would also lend
assistance in reviving the historic role of Richard Nixon
and his presidency is truly a marvel.

In 1979, Richard Nixon was asked to mediate the US
professional baseball league strike. Black Republican
businessmen hosted a dinner to honor Richard Nixon in 1985.
Newsweek called Nixon, the "sage of Saddle River" in 1986.

The Nation described the "latest new Nixon" in 1986. No
less than the governor of New York suggested in early 1987
that Richard Nixon be named the chief US negotiator for arms
limitation due to his skill in handling the Soviet diplomats
while president. This resurfacing of the Nixon mystique has
been noted across university campuses, where the Nixon
presidency is presented more favorably than a decade earlier
and praised for its accomplishments in comparison to more
recent presidential administrations. Through this new
emphasis and understanding of the Nixon presidency's
accomplishments, the Watergate scandal is presently viewed
as a flaw that tragically ended an otherwise brilliant
presidential administration. Richard Nixon, thus, has
achieved another resurrection in American politics.

Books

1688.   Korff, Bernard. The Personal Nixon: Staying on the
        Summit. Washington, DC: Fairness Publishers,
        1974.

1689.   Lasky, Victor. It Didn't Start with Watergate. New
        York, NY: Dell Publishing Co., 1977.

1690.   Marvell, Charles. In Defense of Nixon: A Study in
        Political Psychology and Political Pathology.
        Albuquerque, NM: American Classical College
        Press, 1976.

1691.   Miller, R.H. The Nixon Haters: How They Did Him
        In. St. Parson, NY: McCain Publishing Co.,
        1975.

1692.   Smith, Franklin B. Assassination of President Nixon.
        New York, NY: Academic Books, 1976.

Journal Articles

1693. Adler, Renata. "Searching for the Real Nixon
      Scandal." Atlantic Monthly 238 (December 1976):
      76-84+.

1694. Brown, Steven R. "Richard Nixon and the Public
      Conscience: The Struggle for Authenticity."
      Journal of Psychohistory 6 (Summer 1976): 93-
      111.

1695. Carlin, David R. "Lament for Richard Nixon."
      America 150 (January 21, 1984): 23-24.

1696. "Citizen Nixon in Peking." Newsweek 87 (March 1,
      1976): 16-17.

1697. Cooper, Arthur. "An Exclusive Interview with Richard
      Nixon." Family Week (December 26, 1982): 4-8.

1698. Foley, Charles. "Richard Nixon's Comeback Plan."
      Observer (October 1875): 16-18.

1699. "The Ghost Walks." Economist 268 (July 15, 1978):
      38.

1700. Glynn, Lenny. "Nixon's New Influence." Macleans 97
      (April 23, 1984): 10-11.

1701. Haag, E. (van den). "A Perversion of the
      Constitution." Skeptic 1 (1975): 11-12.

1702. Hoffman, Nicholas (von). "How Nixon Got Strung Up."
      New Republic 187 (June 25, 1982): 24-27.

1703. Horner, Charles. "Hindsight." Commentary 70 (August
      1980): 64-65.

1704. Kitman, M. "Springtime for Nixon." New Leader 67
      (May 28, 1984): 22-23.

1705. "The Latest New Nixon." Nation 242 (January 25,
      1986): 65.

1706. Mee, J.R. "A Sufficient Body of Evidence." Skeptic
      1 (1975): 13-14.

1707. Neuchterlein, James A. "Watergate: Toward a
      Revisionist View." Commentary 68 (August 1979):
      38-45.

1708.   "Nixon Comes Back into the Limelight--and
        Controversy."   US News and World Report 80 (March
        1, 1976):   24.

1709.   "Nixon Speaks." Newsweek 89 (April 9, 1977):   35-39.

1710.   "The Nixon Special."   Nation 224 (February 26, 1977):
        228.

1711.   "Nixon's Fourth Comeback." National Review 30
        (December 22, 1978):   1579-1580.

1712.   Overland, Doris.   "They Killed a Man." Contemporary
        Review 228 (June 1979):   313-318.

1713.   "The Real Nixon."   Time 116 (June 9, 1980):   22.

1714.   "Richard Nixon Calling." Newsweek 96 (December 29,
        1980):   15.

1715.   Riesman, David.   "Attitudes Toward President Nixon:
        A Case of American Exceptionalism in Relation to
        Watergate." Tocqueville Review 4 (Fall/Winter
        1982):   280-302.

1716.   Rosenfield, Laurence W.   "August 9, 1974:   The
        Victimage of Richard Nixon." Communication
        Quarterly 24 (Fall 1976):   19-23.

1717.   Rovere, Richard.   "Richard the Bold." New Yorker 54
        (June 19, 1978):   96-97.

1718.   Slansky, Paul.   "Why Not the Worst? Nixon in 1979."
        Politics Today 6 (July 1976):   42-46.

1719.   Sprague, Richard E.   "Nixon, Ford, and the Political
        Assassination in the United States." Computers
        and People 24 (January 1975):   27-31.

1720.   "The Unreal Statesman." Economist 275 (May 24,
        1980):   117.

Author

Richard Nixon is also an author. Since his resignation
of the presidency in 1974, he has written five books and
several journal articles. Earlier in his political career,
Nixon had written a memoir detailing six important events in
his career to that time. The work was entitled Six Crises
(1962), and it received favorable reviews. Authorship
creates a new image for Richard Nixon. The critics so far
have been divided on the success of this new Nixon. In
nearly all cases, reviewers have labelled Nixon's work as
interesting and even fascinating. A reasonable argument can
be made that Richard Nixon does have some literary ability.

Unfortunately for Nixon, there has also been a
consensus among reviewers that his books have been self-
serving, factually erratic, and basically polemics. One
reviewer labelled his No More Vietnams (1985) as nothing
more than a morning diatribe. Real War (1980) was found to
contain oversimplifcations and misstatements. Though RN
(1978) was fascinating reading, most reviewers still found
the work to be highly selective of the events discussed and
undeniably an ego trip for the author. The lack of
documentation of Nixon's works has been noted by all
reviewers. One critic maintained that the information

contained in Real War (1980) has to be accepted on faith
alone. Such criticisms of Nixon's books do much to diminish
the otherwise interesting narrative in each. Nixon's books
are not products of academic scholarship. But, they are
useful supplements to the body of literature available
concerning Richard Nixon and his presidency. They do form,
however weak, the "other" side in the continuing public
opinion battle for Nixon's place in history.

Books

1721. Six Crises. New York, NY: Doubleday, 1962.

> Richard Nixon provides an annount of his fourteen
> years in public service as congressman and then
> vice-president. He details the Hiss case, the
> Caracas Incident, the Kitchen Debate in Moscow, and
> the 1960 presidential election campaign.

Reviews

> American Political Science Review 56 (September 1962):
> 735
>
> Booklist 58 (May 1, 1962): 602
>
> Bookmark 21 (May 1962): 221
>
> Chicago Sunday Tribune (April 8, 1962): 1
>
> Christian Century 79 (June 6, 1962): 720
>
> Christian Science Monitor (March 29, 1962): 11
>
> Foreign Affairs 40 (July 1962): 668
>
> Library Journal 87 (April 15, 1962): 1600
>
> New Republic 146 (April 9, 1962): 22
>
> New York Herald Tribune (April 1, 1962): 5.

New York Times Book Review (April 1, 1962): 3

Political Science Quarterly 77 (September 1962): 414

San Francisco Chronicle (April 1, 1962): 28

Spectator (October 5, 1962): 520

Springfield Republican (April 8, 1962): 4D

Times Literary Supplement (October 1962): 771

1722. RN, the Memories of Richard Nixon. New York, NY:
      Grossett, 1978.

      Richard Nixon provides here his version of the
momentous events of his presidency: US involvement
in Vietnam, the China visit, negotiations with the
Soviets, and, of course, Watergate. This work is
autobiographical and serves as a recent presidential
history for the Nixon presidency.

Reviews

      Book World (May 28, 1978): 1+

      Booklist 74 (July 15, 1978): 1714

      Choice 15 (December 1978): 1435

      Christian Century 95 (September 13, 1978): 836

      Christian Science Monitor (June 21, 1978): 18

      Kirkus Review 46 (May 15, 1978): 588

      Library Journal 103 (July 1978): 1383

      Nation 227 (July 8/15, 1978): 53

      National Review 30 (August 18, 1978): 1031

      New Statesman 95 (June 9, 1978): 775

      New York Review of Books 25 (June 29, 1978): 3

      New York Times Books Review (June 11, 1978): 1

New Yorker 54 (June 19, 1978): 96

Progressive 42 (August 1978): 39-41

Times Literary Supplement (July 7, 1978): 759

1723. The Real War. New York, NY: Warner Books, 1980.

Richard Nixon, reverting to an anticommunist approach
to the Soviet Union as opposed to detente, argues the
methods for best management of world power in face of
the Soviet threat in this work.

Reviews

Christian Science Monitor (June 18, 1980): 17

Commentary 70 (August 1980): 64

Critic 39 (October 1980): 3

Economist 275 (May 24, 1980): 117

Library Journal 105 (July 1980): 1494

National Review 32 (July 25, 1980): 908

New Republic 182 (June 14, 1980): 32

New York Review of Books 27 (June 26, 1980): 18

New York Times Book Review (May 25, 1980): 7

Saturday Review 7 (June 1980): 67

1724. Leaders. New York, NY: Warner Books, 1982.

Nixon analyzes in this set of brief biographical
profiles world leaders whom he considers as shapers
of the modern world. Among the world leaders
described are Churchill, Krushchev, and Chou Enlai.

Reviews

>   Christian Science Monitor (October 27, 1982):   15
>
>   Library Journal 107 (December 15, 1982):   2334
>
>   National Review 35 (February 4, 1983):   135
>
>   Political Science Quarterly 98 (Fall 1983):   513
>
>   Times Literary Supplement (March 25, 1983):   287

1725. Real Peace. Boston, MA: Little, Brown, and Company,
       1984.

>   In this work, Richard Nixon defines real peace as
>   absence of overt aggression between the United States
>   and the Soviet Union. The methods offered by Nixon
>   to maintain real peace are summitry, economic ties,
>   and linkage.

Reviews

>   American Spectator 17 (May 1984):   33
>
>   Booklist 80 (January 15, 1984):   697
>
>   Christian Science Monitor 75 (September 1983):   38
>
>   Kirkus Review 51 (December 1, 1983):   1246
>
>   Library Journal 109 (March 1, 1984):   496
>
>   National Review 36 (February 24, 1984):   50
>
>   New York Times Book Review (January 29, 1984):   6

1726. No More Vietnams. New York, NY: Arbor House, 1985.

>   Richard Nixon presents in this work his version of
>   the actions taken to end U.S. involvement in the
>   Vietnamese War. Presenting the history of U.S.
>   involvement in Vietnam from the Truman administration
>   through the Paris Peace Accords of 1973, Nixon argues
>   that the United States won the war but lost the peace
>   through congressional refusal to supply money and
>   equipment when needed in the early 1970s.

Reviews

    American Spectator 18 (May 1985): 29

    Booklist 81 (March 1, 1985): 891

    Christian Century 102 (August 28, 1985): 775

    Foreign Affairs 63 (Fall 1985): 919

    Kirkus Review 53 (February 1, 1985): 133

    Library Journal 110 (April 1, 1985): 145

    National Review 37 (May 3, 1985): 52

    New Republic 192 (June 10, 1985): 29

    New York Review of Books 32 (May 30, 1985): 11

    New York Time Book Review (April 7, 1985): 5

    Policy Review (Summer 1985): 87

Periodical Articles

1727.   "Application of the Inherent Danger Doctrine to
         Servants of Negligent Independent Contractors."
         Duke Bar Association Journal 4 (Spring 1936).

1728.   "Asia After Vietnam." Foreign Affairs 46 (October
         1967): 111-125.

1729.   "Changing Rules of Liability in Automobile Accident
         Litigation." Duke University Law and
         Constitutional Problems 3 (1936).

1730.   "Cuba, Castro, and John F. Kennedy." Reader's Digest
         85 (November 1964): 281-284+.

1731.   "Four Academic Freedoms." Saturday Review 49 (August
         27, 1966): 12-13+.

1732.   "The Greater Menace." Educational Record 39 (January
         1958).

1733. "Hard-Headed Detente." New York Times Magazine 131
      (August 1982): A21.

1734. "Khruschev's Hidden Weaknesses." Saturday Evening
      Post 236 (October 12, 1963): 23-29.

1735. "Lessons of the Alger Hiss Case." Human Events 46
      (March 15, 1986): 10-12.

1736. "Let's Give Business a Square Deal." Nation's
      Business 54 (April 1966): 46-47+.

1737. "Needed in Vietnam: The Will to Win." Reader's
      Digest 85 (August 1964): 37-43.

1738. "On Economic Power." New York Times Magazine 131
      (August 1982): A27.

1739. "Plea for an Anti-communist Faith." Saturday Review
      of Literature (March 24, 1952): 12-13.

1740. "Strange Case of Alger Hiss." Reader's Digest 81
      (November 1962): 88-93+.

1741. "Super Power Summitry." Foreign Affairs 65 (Fall
      1985): 1-11.

1742. "Unforgettable John Foster Dulles." Reader's Digest
      91 (July 1967): 99-104.

1743. "What Has Happened to America?" Reader's Digest 91
      (October 1967): 49-54.

1744. "Why Not Negotiate in Vietnam?" Reader's Digest 87
      (December 1965): 49-54.